"A must-read for those who are stressed or anxious, or those who are near the stressed and anxious, which is to say, all of us. Drawing from everything from Descartes to polyvagal theory to Zelda, Charles Schaeffer's approach is as entertaining as it is informative. It is not an overstatement to say that this work will change lives."

—**Mary Pilon**, *New York Times* bestselling
author of *The Monopolists*, *The Kevin Show*,
and *The Longest Race*

"Charles Schaeffer has broken important ground in synthesizing polyvagal theory and cutting-edge neuroscience with concrete applications of techniques that give people experiencing panic the tools to better understand themselves, manage their issues, and thrive. Learning more about the power of how you relate to yourself in an interpersonal context translates to a superpower, and this book gives you the recipe to make the transformation!"

—**Daniel Singley, PhD**, founding director
of the Center for Men's Excellence, and
coauthor of *Parental Mental Health*

T0000966

WHEN PAN!C HAPPENS

**Short-Circuit Anxiety & Fear in the Moment
Using Neuroscience & Polyvagal Theory**

CHARLES SCHAEFFER, PHD

New Harbinger Publications, Inc.

Publisher's Note

NEW HARBINGER PUBLICATIONS is a registered trademark of New Harbinger Publications, Inc.

New Harbinger Publications is an employee-owned company.

Copyright © 2024 by Charles Schaeffer
New Harbinger Publications, Inc.
5720 Shattuck Avenue
Oakland, CA 94609
www.newharbinger.com
All Rights Reserved

Cover design by Sara Christian; Interior design by Michele Waters-Kermes;
Acquired by Wendy Millstine and Jennye Garibaldi;
Edited by Elizabeth Dougherty

Library of Congress Cataloging-in-Publication Data on file

Printed in the United States of America

26   25   24

10   9   8   7   6   5   4   3   2   1   First Printing

Contents

PART 3: Keep Your Nervous System Calm and Stable

PART 1

Discover What Happens When You Panic

CHAPTER 1

Explore Your Nervous System

Problems controlling nausea, a racing heart, and other panic symptoms are shared by millions of people, like you, worldwide. This book provides quick exercises and ongoing practices grounded in neuroscience and leading clinical psychotherapies to stop and prevent panic attacks, panic symptoms, and anxiety. With patience, practice, and acceptance, you can reset your nervous system and ease your struggle with panic. Whether this is the first book you've picked up for help with your panic or the hundredth, you can overcome the struggle by consistently applying and using these exercises and practices.

Each chapter offers interactive exercises based in neuropsychology. Try the exercises at your own pace and use the most helpful ones as needed. Even just looking at a chapter when you're struggling is a powerful commitment to helping yourself live with less panic and anxiety. Millions of people struggle with anxiety and panic. Yet, only a few will do something as profoundly compassionate as learning to use their nervous systems to feel safe and secure.

You can read the chapters in order for a more linear understanding of your nervous system. You can also jump around based on what interests you. The most important advice for using this book is to practice the exercises consistently and to the best of your ability. Consistency, patience, and practice will help you restore your balance at a neurological level and overcome panic and anxiety symptoms more effectively every day. One of the best ways to use this book is to choose one or two exercises that you think could be helpful to you and practice them a few times over a few weeks. It may be beneficial to try an exercise multiple times before deciding whether or not it works for you. The most important thing is to find the exercises that best fit your unique circumstances. Take your time— even opening this book and reading this far takes you a step closer to regaining your calm and overcoming panic. Be proud that you've started.

★ Dan's Story

Dan feels like he is going to throw up. His heart is racing. His mind can't seem to focus on one thought. He feels a cold, tingly sensation on the tops of his hands as he prepares his notes for a team presentation. Dan, a business analyst at a startup company, has presented to many people before, but today he can't seem to shake his intense worry. He knows he didn't sleep well but has no idea what is happening inside his body and mind. He feels robbed of his confidence and competency to present. His mind goes blank. He feels frozen for what feels like hours, but is actually minutes, before he begins his presentation. Dan is able to white-knuckle through the presentation while feeling waves of what he thinks might be panic. A quick Reddit search reveals a lot of funny memes about panic attacks. The 171 million search results on Google overwhelm him because it's impossible to know what information is reliable.

Dan can't sleep. It's been about a week since he experienced what he thinks was his first panic attack before the presentation. He watched hours of TikTok videos and even tried a meditation app, but he still feels stuck and worried. The worry keeps him up at *night. Pins and needles run up and down the back of his spine when he lies in bed and tries to sleep. Dan spends his nights imagining each nauseous moment of having another panic attack at work, even the sweat gathering on his palms. He's usually confident and has never felt this hopeless or lost. Dan's always prided himself on his ability to think through things, but now his thoughts seem to betray him, leaving him demoralized and exhausted.*

How often have you felt like Dan?

Your Operating System and Panic

Like Dan, you have an inner, unconscious system. It's similar to the operating system of an electronic device, running to help you function and survive in life. When you are struck by panic and anxiety symptoms, like Dan, something in that system is out of balance. Without your awareness or knowledge, these underlying systems are deep within your body and nervous system. They are known as the autonomic nervous system.

When your heart rate slows or speeds up as you work out in the gym, when you drift unconscious to fall asleep, even when you sigh or yawn, you have experienced your autonomic nervous system doing its job. It's always in the background of your conscious experiences, balancing signals in your body, so you can optimally work and relate to others in your environment without becoming over-whelmed (Porges 2011).

Panic sensations, like nausea and a racing heart, mean that a part of your nervous system is overwhelmed and needs to be brought back into balance. When you are bal-anced internally, you can feel safe to engage with, provide empathy for, and draw empathy from others. This is our preferred way of being as a social, interpersonal species (Porges 2022; Porges and Dana 2018). Decades of research from neurologists and psychologists have shown us that the nervous system is wired to the largest nerve in our bodies, the vagus nerve. Together they make up the *poly-vagal system*. The vagus nerve underlies our ability to connect and feel understood by others. The ability to empathize and connect to others in order to discharge some of your pain and regulate strong emotions, like fear and sadness, is called *coregulation*.

Polyvagal theory is a neuroscience theory that all of your emotional, social, and individual experiences are regulated by your unconscious nervous system. This means your unconscious nervous system is constantly running in the background without you having to think about it, flowing through the same three interlocking branches of your vagus nerve. This is called your *polyvagal system*. When your polyvagal system is in balance, you can remain resilient and stay connected to others even when you feel anxious or scared—this is one of the greatest strengths of the human race (Porges 2022; Porges 2011). Balancing your polyvagal system requires its three interlocking parts to align and work well with each other. When they don't, you lose your sense of safety and can experience uncomfortable panic sensations in your body, like Dan did.

Balancing Parts of the Nervous System

Your polyvagal system is similar to the Triforce in the classic game *The Legend of Zelda*. This mystical force consistently guides and protects the hero, Link, on his journey to overcome dangerous and scary threats. It consists of three separate triangles of power, that when combined, allow players to conquer evil forces and restore balance. Each part is individually powerful but most effective when combined with the others.

Similarly, when you're rescuing yourself from panic and anxiety in everyday life, you rely on three powers that work together. According to polyvagal theory, your nervous system uses three interlocking neurological branches of the vagus nerve, known as the *dorsal vagal*, *sympathetic*, and *ventral vagal*, to help you deal with and overcome stress. Each of these branches serves its own purpose, helping you adapt and interact with your environment and other people.

- The *dorsal vagal* branch is in charge of slowing down your breathing, reducing your heart rate, disconnecting you from other people, and allowing you to focus on your own experience.

- The *sympathetic* branch is in charge of speeding up your heart rate, using your senses to scan for safety or danger in your environment, and preparing your body and brain for fight or flight.

- The *ventral vagal* branch coordinates the messages among the three vagus nerve branches. This coordination activates your empathy and ability to engage with others, enabling you to talk, interact, support, and generally help others tolerate strong emotions and sensations without becoming overwhelmed, a.k.a. coregulation (Dana 2020; Porges and Dana 2018).

While your polyvagal system is engaged, a subconscious process called *neuroception* uses your senses to constantly check and scan internally and externally for threats and danger, so you can feel balanced and able to engage with other people moment to moment (Porges 2011). Neuroception acts like a firewall against environmental stress.

Panic happens when you become locked in the sympathetic nervous system. Your *sympathetic nervous system* is the set of nerves throughout your body that carry signals for fight-or-flight responses mobilizing you to take quick action. Fight-or-flight responses are signals sent through your sympathetic nervous system that increase your heart rate, muscle tension, and blood flow to prepare you to survive dangerous or threatening situations by fighting or running away. This book largely focuses on using the rest of your nervous system to rebalance your nervous system and prevent or stop panic and fight-or-flight sensations and symptoms, such as a racing heart rate, shortness of breath, nausea, racing thoughts, and muscle tension.

Let's take a look at how Dan experiences this. When his panic happens, Dan struggles to feel heard or find words. He loses balance in his nervous system as his sympathetic nervous system is activated, sending waves of uncomfortable sensations to his stomach and increasing his heart rate. His dorsal vagal branch fails to slow down his breathing and heart rate or disconnect him from the experiences of his body, nor is he capable of engaging with other people to help him calm down and think. His system continues to scan for threats and danger through neuroception, sending more adrenaline and signals for action into his body.

Like Dan, when panic strikes, you might also get stuck, unable to engage the other branches of your polyvagal system and restore balance to your internal Triforce. However, through neurological exercises and practices, you can overcome panic by finding a way back to balance. Here are some exercises that can help you become more aware of your nervous system and help you restore balance when you feel stuck in panic and anxiety.

What Your Breath Tells You

When you're *mindful*, you accept the present moment as is without judgment. In this state of acceptance, you can better tolerate uncomfortable feelings, like panic and anxiety. A great way to build acceptance and awareness of how your nervous system affects you is by tracking your breath (Dana 2020; Linehan 2014).

Your breath, without trying to change it or alter it in any way, indicates where you might be stuck in your nervous system. Here are some ways to describe how your breath reflects the state of your nervous system:

- **BALANCED:** When your breath is deep, strong, long, and intentional, your nervous system is telling you it is in balance and able to interact and coregulate strong emotions, like panic, with others.

- **DISCONNECTED:** When your breath is flat, weak, or difficult, your nervous system is telling you that you're likely out of balance and feeling disconnected, out of it, or distant from others.

- **ANXIOUS:** When your breath is shallow, quick, or uncontrollable, the signals for fight and flight are taking over. Your sympathetic nervous system is activated, and everything and everyone can feel like a threat. This is where you may experience panic and anxiety symptoms, such as a racing heart, shortness of breath, or nausea.

By observing your breath and thinking about how it reflects different states of your nervous system, you can better anticipate times when you might be at risk of experiencing panic and anxiety. This next exercise can help you be better able to head off or respond more quickly to symptoms.

Try This **Track Your Breath**

Over the next week, note any time you catch your breath shifting. You can use a notebook or a text app to record what happens. This activity is called breath tracking. If it's easier, you can assess your breath at breakfast, lunch, and dinner.

Write down the context (where you are and what you're doing), the time of day, and anything else you think might be helpful in making sense of how your breath changes over time.

Next, apply one of the following labels to your observations: balanced, disconnected, or anxious. For example, Dan finds before meetings his breathing is shallow, quick, and impulsive, so he labels this "anxious." Later, when he's out to dinner with his friends, he notices his breath is deep, long, and powerful, so he labels this "balanced."

At the end of a week of tracking, review your notes and look for any patterns, for example, any contexts that carry the same label more than three times. Ask yourself:

- What does this pattern tell me about how I feel in this context?

- What is surprising about this?

- What is relieving about this?

- How do I feel about this context now?

Movements That Reconnect You

Most of your body is connected to your polyvagal system through your vagus nerve, where 80 percent of information and sensations travels back and forth from your body to your brain. This connection is a two-way street, meaning that specific movements in your body can activate your vagus nerve, creating reconnection to your nervous system. Some movements can even restart your nervous system to allow for reconnection when your nervous system is overwhelmed or out of balance (Rosenberg 2017; Porges 2011; Dana 2020).

The following exercise utilizes body and eye movements to physically reset the polyvagal system. This can offer relief when you are stuck in panic symptoms, like nausea, a racing heart, a cold sweat, or pins and needles on your skin.

Connectivity Repair

This is not a cognitive exercise and requires no thinking what-soever. Try this exercise at a time when you are feeling acti-vated and anxious.

Start by finding a place where you can lie flat on your back. Take note of your breath and any tension in your body.

Next, interweave the fingers of both hands and support the back of your head with them. Keeping your head still and in your hands, have your eyes look as far right as they can. Don't move your head, just your eyes.

Continue to look far right for thirty to ninety seconds, until you involuntarily yawn, swallow, or sigh. These involuntary reactions signal that you have reconnected the parts of your polyvagal system.

Repeat this process by looking to your left as far as you can without moving your head. Again wait thirty to ninety seconds, until you involuntarily yawn, swallow, or sigh.

Before you sit up, take a moment to notice any change in your breath or tension in your body. You can practice this exercise whenever you notice panic symptoms, like your heart racing or shallow breathing.

Body-Scan Meditation

A body-scan meditation is another way to rebalance your nervous system and decrease panic symptoms. It can be relaxing to practice this exercise when you aren't experiencing panic or anxiety symptoms. The more you practice it the easier and more natural it will feel—and the more effective it can be when you're dealing with panic symptoms.

Place a yoga mat or blanket on the floor. Lie down flat on your back. Close your eyes.

Breathe in deeply for four seconds. Hold your breath for two seconds. Breathe out for five seconds. Continue this breathing pattern for five cycles before letting your breath settle, using no effort to control it.

Scan your body starting at your toes and slowly moving up the parts of your body. Feel for any tension along the way. Perhaps in your legs? Back? Neck? Jaw? Eyes?

Repeat the breathing pattern—breathe in for four seconds, hold for two seconds, and out for five seconds—a total of ten times. As you inhale, imagine you are gently pulling out tension. Imagine your exhale is a warm cloud surrounding wherever you are tense.

When you're done, open your eyes, take a moment, and reflect on these questions:

- What feels different in my body now compared to before I started?

- What is surprising about this?

- What is calming about this?

- What is empowering about this?

Takeaways

In this chapter, you learned how panic and anxiety arise when your nervous system is out of balance or stuck.

Your nervous system is intertwined with the vagal nerve. This intertwining makes up the vagal system. Among its functions, the vagal nerve underlies your ability to connect and feel understood by others.

You can't consciously sense or control the actions of the nervous system or the vagal nerve. However, through exercises based in neuropsychology, you can influence and reduce symptoms that they cause, for example, a racing heart or shallow breathing that accompanies panic.

You learned targeted exercises to help you notice, short out, and reduce panic as you are experiencing it. You learned to combat panic symptoms at a neurological level using your breath, your eyes, and your mind as they happen. You're already more able to combat your panic using your nervous system.

CHAPTER 2

Respond to Overwhelming Panic and Anxiety

The spinning wheel of death on your laptop. The red blinking light on your game player. The text frozen on your work computer and the oh-so-helpful message "application not responding." You likely know what it looks like when a device becomes overwhelmed and crashes. You probably also know how frustrating and terrifying that moment can be before you are able to reboot and recover. It is much harder to understand, respond, and recover when your nervous system becomes overwhelmed. If racing thoughts, dizziness, nausea, or muscle tension immobilize you, it helps to investigate what typically causes your nervous system to crash. More importantly, you can learn how to recover from panic.

When a tech device crashes, what's the first thing to do? You might notice that you lose cellular or Wi-Fi connectivity, for example—which is similar to what happens when your nervous system crashes. When you become overwhelmed with panic symptoms, your brain retreats into a safety mode, cutting off connectivity to the environment, other people, and even empathy. You experience increased vigilance and distancing. Recovering from nervous system crashes relies on you feeling safe. Until you can perceive and experience safety, you're likely to remain stuck in this anxious, activated mode of responding to yourself and others. Generally, the safer you can feel, the easier and faster your nervous system recovers and returns to a sense of calm and balance.

The *vagal brake* is a built-in tool for calming your nervous system (for example, by decreasing your heart and breathing rate) and recovering when you are overwhelmed and anxious. While there is no one specific physical vagal break, it generally refers to the part of your brain where the vagus nerve begins deep in the back of your head, near your brain stem. Your vagal brake is like brakes on a bicycle. It releases to speed up the nervous system and reengages to slow it down (Dana 2020). This is your main mechanism of getting back to calm when you lose your sense of connection to others and begin to feel overwhelmed and threatened with panic symptoms. When your heart rate slows, that's a sign that your vagal brake is working. One way to overcome panic and anxiety and balance and calm your nervous system is by learning to engage your vagal brake. The exercises in this chapter will help you explore this.

★ *Gloria's Story*

Gloria stopped eating breakfast because she didn't want to keep throwing up in third period. Since returning to teaching postpandemic, after a year of lockdowns and remote teaching, Gloria, a seventh-grade history teacher, couldn't shake her daily cold sweats and nausea around students. While she had taken steps to protect her health, she continues to worry about contracting the flu or COVID from students, flinching whenever she hears a loud cough or sneeze. During her lesson-planning period, she almost always gets uncomfortable waves of pins and needles down her spine and can't seem to focus on anything but the humiliating thought of throwing up in public. While she has been able to white-knuckle through her feelings and sensations for a couple of weeks, her focus and teaching has taken a hit. Her goal is to feel "okay at school" again.

Gloria notices that most of her panic and anxiety symptoms (nausea, pins and needles down her spine, involuntary flinching) disconnect her from feeling in control and calm in her body.

Have you ever felt like Gloria? Have you lost control and crashed your nervous system into panic mode? Each of these uncomfortable sensations is signaling adrenaline and cortisol to pump through your nervous system as it prepares for a threat. Activating your vagal brake can help you not get stuck in this fight-or-flight response, a.k.a. survival mode. Survival mode happens when your nervous system becomes overwhelmed with adrenaline and sends uncomfortable panic sensations through your body, pushing you to engage with aggression (fight) or flee in fear (flight).

How do you reconnect with your body when you get stuck in survival mode? How do you stop panic sensations like a rapid heartbeat, shallow breathing, nausea, and overall feelings of dread? Practices like the body-integration scan, described below, rewire responses to panic, reducing and eliminating intense, uncomfortable panic sensations

(Creswell et al. 2016). The body-integration scan is helpful when you notice your heart beating rapidly, your breath becoming shallower and shorter, or pins and needles running up and down the back of your neck. The body-integration scan has been shown to help restore balance when your nervous system is stuck in survival mode.

I recommend making this exercise a daily practice. If you do it each morning, for example, you will feel an overall release of body tension and an increase in calm and focus. Practicing the body-integration scan over months will change your nervous system, increasing your ability to quickly calm down and focus.

Try This Body-Integration Scan

Settle into a comfortable position, either sitting or lying down. Close your eyes and take a few deep breaths. Follow the visualization steps below slowly. Aim for about ten to fifteen minutes to complete the exercise.

Imagine a beam of light starting at the top of your head going all the way through your body and down to the base of your feet.

Imagine looking into your toes and scan for any sensations in your toes and feet. Notice any tension or points where your foot is relaxed. Are your feet tired and sore? At ease and calm? You might notice your mind starting to drift away to other thoughts. Return your thoughts to picturing the beam of light and bring your attention back to your feet. Remain there for a moment before moving your attention up your legs.

Following the light up from your feet, move your attention to your ankles, then to your calves, shins, thighs, and then finally up into your hips. Scan each area slowly with your mind, using the image of the beam of light to anchor your thoughts. Note any sensations along the way. Do you notice tightness or looseness? Any other sensations? Whatever they might be, don't try to change them. Simply continue to guide your mind as your attention follows the light from your hips to your stomach, chest, and back.

Notice if your breath is deep or shallow. Notice how your heart beats as you scan over it. Become aware of any tension or tightness in your lower and upper back. Rather than trying to change anything, simply observe and connect each area to the next one following the ray of light.

Next, guide your attention to your shoulders, into your neck, around the back of your head, across your forehead, and over your eyes, nose, ears, and mouth, and down to your chin. Continue to notice any sensations. Are you feeling loose or tight in your jaw? Are your shoulders tight? Whatever you may notice, again attempt to not change or alter it in any way—simply observe and connect each part following the beam of light.

Finally, turn your attention back to your toes. Observe and follow the light, noticing how it connects every part of your body that you just scanned. Take a moment to mentally imagine each part connecting from toes to head. Spend a few moments focusing your awareness on your entire body connected as a whole.

When you open your eyes, take a moment and reflect on the following questions:

- What feels different in my body now compared to before I started?

- What feels easier in my body, for example, breathing?

- What is calming about this?

- What is empowering about this?

Gloria uses the body-integration scan before school and right before her first class each day. Within a week, she reports being able to focus more clearly again. However, she notices the nausea continuing after classes, once she has completed teaching. This isn't uncommon. Digestive functions and signals are directly connected to the vagus nerve. Everyday work and life stressors can often tire out your nervous system, leaving lingering symptoms of anxiety and stress, for example, in your gut.

Let's look at another practice drawn from polyvagal theory: the calm anchor playlist. In the Netflix series *Stranger Things*, the main characters are faced with a lot of creepy villains from the bizzarro universe, the "Upside Down." None are as terrifying as Vecna. Vecna can overtake people's minds, driving them insane to the point of death. When it seems that all hope is lost, the heroes discover that consciously focusing on music that makes them feel loved and safe repels and eventually defeats Vecna. According to polyvagal theory, the kids from *Stranger Things* defeated Vecna by using music as an anchor for safety. This engaged their vagal brake to restore their balance and keep out panic and Vecna. This same approach works for panic attacks.

The following exercise is an adapted version of a popular distress-tolerance practice foundational to dialectical behavior therapy (DBT) treatment and skills programs (Linehan 2014). DBT is a type of psychotherapy for people who experience intense, distressing emotions. You can practice this exercise to strengthen your vagal brake whenever you'd like. You can use it to calm your nervous system when you feel panicked.

Try This — Calm Anchor Playlist

Make a playlist of a few songs that bring you peace, calm, and positive memories. Listen to them as you make the playlist and notice how your body feels.

Find a comfortable, private spot where you won't be disturbed for five to ten minutes. Sit in a comfortable position, uncross your arms, and hold your palms comfortably open facing the ceiling as they rest on your lap.

Consciously notice any tension in your face. Try to release it and keep your mouth pursed in a half smile as you breathe through your nose.

Start your calming anchor playlist and close your eyes, intentionally holding a half smile with your palms open and facing up. When your mind drifts to other thoughts or feelings, gently bring your attention back to the song, your half smile, and your palms.

After each song is completed, observe and notice any different sensations in your mind or body. Do you notice any change in tension or stress?

Gloria adds the calm anchor playlist exercise to her after-class routine. Within a month, she reports feeling minimal anxiety and no nausea when in school. She is able to switch easily from being activated in fight-or-flight mode into a calmer state. Her ability to engage her vagal brake to stop adrenaline and panic has become very strong. By the end of the year, Gloria wins the distinguished teaching award at her school and gives her acceptance speech over a stack of pancakes at the PTA appreciation brunch.

Takeaways

Practicing the exercises in this chapter will help you build your nervous system's effectiveness to calm you and stop panic sensations at a neurological level. Over time, consistent practice of these exercises will increase your resilience to stress, anxiety, and panic. The following chapters offer more exercises to strengthen your nervous system in order to help you reduce panic and discomfort, while at the same time building resilience.

CHAPTER 3

Defuse Anxious Thoughts and Rumination

It's all in your head. Mind over matter. Think your way out of it. These are examples of the various frustrating and demoralizing messages and advice many people have received to address their panic and anxiety. This simplistic model dominates many self-help books and coaching seminars, but it is not entirely inaccurate. The things in your head, a.k.a. thoughts or internal narration, can overwhelm your nervous system, throwing you into panic and inaction.

Your conscious mind is like an email inbox constantly being sent messages from your internal and external worlds. Sorting these emails, deciding which are worth reading, which are junk, and which are dangerous viruses, is a difficult task. There's no organic spam filter, firewall, or antivirus program for the messages your mind sends us. They can act like computer viruses, generating panic and anxiety. You wouldn't open and read every random email in your spam folder. Yet, it's common to continue to treat every thought that enters the brain as safe to open and bring into the nervous system.

One of the first steps in developing an internal filter and firewall for thoughts related to panic and anxiety is understanding the ways you interact with thoughts that increase panic symptoms. You may have developed patterns of thinking and engaging with your thoughts that disturb and throw off your polyvagal system, throwing you into worse panic. Common patterns that create this inability to regulate your emotional responses are rumination and cognitive fusion.

Rumination is the process of perpetually reviewing and processing the same anxious or uncertain thought—like malware in your computer's processor. Rumination hijacks all your attention and focuses it on a scary or panic-related thought, potentially until you crash. Rumination is a great indicator that you are stuck in fight-or-flight mode, with your sympathetic nervous system scanning for threats.

Thousands of years of evolution have made the brain very good at filling in blanks and searching for patterns in the environment when you get stuck on anything uncertain or confusing. However, the brain is not great at letting uncertain thoughts go. If you've ever been consumed by worry about how well you'll do when studying for a test or whether you locked all your doors at home after leaving for a trip, you know what it feels like when your brain won't let go of uncertain thoughts.

Cognitive fusion is the tendency to get caught up in personalizing thought content, as if it were more useful and essential to make sense of your feelings and sensations than anything else. You may not know if you locked every door before a ten-day vacation, but when you use feelings of dread to steer your attention to all the ways your house could be robbed, you are engaged in cognitive fusion. Suddenly, random anxious and worried thoughts and feelings can crowd out your experience of anything else as your heart begins to beat faster and harder—doesn't sound like much a vacation does it? Many people who get caught in cognitive fusion report not only do they get stuck in the same thoughts and predictions (rumination), but they also tend to believe these thoughts as if they were prophecy or truth, rather than just more junk mail from your brain to be put in the trash folder. Finding ways to identify, label, and stop rumination and cognitive fusion is one of the keys to bringing your nervous systems back into balance and reducing panic.

★ Ming's Story

Ming has never found a problem he can't think his way out of, but he can't seem to think of a way to stop the panic attacks. He is one of the youngest senior recruiters at a well-known tech giant and hasn't worried about panic attacks since college. In college, he was able to overcome panic by getting in touch with nature and reconnecting to the things he loved from childhood, such as swimming at a local reef with his family. Last month, he felt like his heart was going to stop, he couldn't catch his breath, and he could barely swim to shore after he had a panic attack while swimming at the reef with his nephew. Ming had another panic attack a week later while on a flight home from New York from a business trip. Since then, he hasn't been able to stop thinking about his next flight or swim, replaying all the ways he might panic again. When he talks about losing the confidence to swim his childhood reef, he cries because it is his primary source of constant relief and calm.

Ming thinks about flying for business or swimming for pleasure and subsequently having a panic attack thirty to forty times a day. When he thinks about a potential panic attack, his heart races, his chest gets very cold, he feels intense warmth flow into his hands and feet, and his mind circles around images and thoughts of having a panic attack and drowning while swimming or "losing his mind" in public on a flight. He constantly worries that his thoughts are warnings about what is to come. His worries start to keep him up at night.

Ming soon learns that he is stuck in a rumination cycle and that when he gets stuck there too long, he experiences cognitive fusion. Ming starts generating predictions about having a panic attack and public embarrassment. His mind imagines humiliating online movies of him having a panic attack on a plane, while everyone in the airport stares and laughs. Soon, Ming can't shake a belief that his anxious thoughts are predictions and reflections of his true self. He's not able to see himself any other way than the embarrassing ruminations he continues to replay in his head. He becomes merged or fused with his thoughts (cognitive fusion). He wants to see things differently, but he can't seem to see anything but embarrassment *and shame in his future. Ming realizes he is getting stuck in his panic symptoms because he can't help but repeatedly imagine and hold on to all the threats his very creative brain can generate. When his thoughts are about business or his family, he can make sense of things. But when he tries to do this with his thoughts about panic attacks, it seems to sabotage him instead.*

Ming needs to find a better way to make sense of and engage with his panic thoughts than rumination and cognitive fusion. Through visual and humorous methods, he applies cognitive defusion—the ability to separate self from thoughts in order to observe them and sort them without the nervous system becoming overwhelmed and entering panic mode. He practices visualization exercises, like the one you will learn next, and tries to find funnier ways to remember his prior panic attacks. He imagines new future scenarios that make him laugh. Ming imagines having a panic attack on a flight where the entire cabin breaks out in a musical number. He imagines feeling like his heart is going to stop on his next swim in the reef and being rescued by a mermaid puppet with giant googly eyes. He practices these exercises daily whenever he notices his thoughts getting stuck on panic. Soon, he reports much less reaction and judgment to thoughts about

swimming and flying. After a month of daily practice,
he resumes his morning swims and books a flight back
to New York.

You can reduce activation of fight-or-flight mode within your nervous system by strengthening your ability to observe and let go of anxious thoughts (Hayes, Strosahl, and Wilson 2011). The following exercise, a self-guided version that I have introduced to many people struggling with rumination and cognitive fusion, can help. You can also find guided versions online and in mental health apps such as Calm.

Try This   Leaves on a Stream

Find a comfortable place to sit for five to ten minutes. Close your eyes.

Visualize sitting next to a stream. It is gently flowing by, bubbling with fresh water. It flows from where you are sitting to farther out into the distance, until it disappears into the horizon.

Notice a leaf floating on top of the water. Watch as the water gently carries the leaf away. The leaf becomes smaller and smaller before it finally disappears with the stream into the horizon. Notice another leaf do this. And another. And another. Each floats down the steam until it disappears into the horizon.

Now imagine you can somehow take a thought, place it on a leaf, and watch it gently float toward the horizon. Allow each new thought to be placed on a leaf and watch it as it floats away. Notice that somehow your thoughts weigh nothing and can easily ride on the leaf all the way into the horizon.

Continue this process, watching each thought get carried off into the distance, farther away from you, down the stream until you can't see it anymore. If you get distracted, observe where your mind went and put that thought on a leaf.

After five to ten minutes, open your eyes and notice any difference in your body, for example, a slower heart rate, deeper breaths, or a quieter pace of thinking.

At the end of practice, open your eyes and ask yourself:

- What feels different in my body now compared to before I started?

- How fast is my thinking now?

- What is relieving about this?

- What is surprising about this?

Leaves on a stream is a cognitive defusion exercise that you can practice daily. Think of it as a daily workout to build your nervous system's ability to relax and become tranquil. When practiced over months, you will notice significant improvement in slowing your heart rate and steadying your breath. After a year, you will find that muscle tension or racing thoughts can pass within minutes or seconds.

Harry Potter's Lesson of Cognitive Defusion

If you're looking to reduce the intensity of your thoughts without daily practice, you can still use cognitive defusion. While leaves on a stream requires a level of seriousness and focus, another cognitive defusion strategy relies on your ability to laugh at yourself—and maybe wield a phoenix feather wand.

One of the first supernatural threats the students at Hogwarts School of Witchcraft and Wizardry learn about is the boggart. The boggart, an immortal boogeyman creature, feeds on people's fear, creating panic in a person and taking on the shape of their greatest fears or nightmares. Thanks to the instruction of the wise Professor Lupin, Harry Potter and his peers learn that laughter and humor repel the boggart. Lupin teaches his students the Riddikulus spell, which requires a wizard to recite the incantation "Riddikulus!" and concentrate on the boggart, consciously changing it into a humorous form. Quickly they learn to find the funny and ridiculous in thoughts, creating deep belly laughs that force the boggart to disappear.

Boggarts have a lot in common with anxiety and panic. If you can find a way to consciously laugh, it creates the safety and space to make them disappear. The Hogwarts students learned to defuse their nightmarish thoughts with conscious humor. This restores their sense of safety, so that their nervous systems can shift out of panic or fight-or-flight mode and repel the boggart. Cognitive defusion can help you let go of, actually separate from, thoughts and feelings. How do you build this panic and regulation skill? The same way every wizard learns to repel dark magic—practice, practice, practice.

When Panic Happens

The key to using humor for cognitive defusion is changing and altering parts of your anxious future thoughts or predictions into something ridiculous and funny. Ming found this strategy to be very effective in helping him take his thoughts less seriously and creating comedic distance from his anxious thoughts. I've also found this strategy very effective for defusing from my own anxious thoughts. For example, as I write my syllabus this afternoon, I may have a catastrophic anxious thought build because this task is important to me as a professor. My thoughts might start with worries that I didn't edit my syllabus perfectly, leading to mistakes that snowball. Suddenly, I'm predicting that these mistakes will result in being fired by my publisher and all my clients, and eventually losing my home because my landlord evicts me. Now if I were to think about it again, going through each thought and interaction step by step but imagining everyone—my university administration, publisher, clients, landlord—are people with wacky, waving inflatable tube arms and googly eyes, the story changes. It's hard to take serious thoughts about being fired by someone with googly eyes and waving inflatable arms.

Humorous Cognitive Defusion

Think of something that scares you and try to make it humorous. Replay each scary prediction in the voice of a cartoon character. With googly eyes. With a really thick accent. Whatever makes you laugh and helps you to defuse from focusing on your anxious thoughts. Doing this allows your brain and nervous system to engage the vagal brake, so you can feel safe, restore balance, and remove panic sensations from your nervous system.

After you replay each situation, ask yourself:

- What feels different in my body now compared to before I started?

- What is surprising about this?

- What is relieving about this?

Takeaways

Using cognitive defusion helps your nervous system overcome scary and anxious thoughts that can trigger panic sensations, including racing thoughts, feelings of dread, nausea, dizziness, an increased heart rate, and difficulty breathing. This chapter describes two cognitive-defusion exercises: imagining leaves on a stream and using humor to make scary thoughts or predictions feel absurd, playful, and approachable. Consistently practicing these exercises will increase your resilience and control over responding to panic-triggered rumination and cognitive fusion. In the next chapter, you will build on this approach by creating solid foundations for stopping and preventing panic by addressing your sleep habits.

CHAPTER 4

Improve Your Sleep

Why do we sleep? What happens if I don't sleep enough? Is that why I get more nervous, more worried, and jumpier? Can insomnia or sleep disruption cause panic symptoms? Make them worse?

These are the kind of questions you might ask when facing sleepless nights while coping with panic and anxiety.

★ *Sara's Story*

Sara is a first-time mom experiencing poor sleep quality since her daughter was born. Sara tosses and turns each night, constantly checking her phone and baby monitor until eventually her heart feels like it is beating out of her chest. She has to jump out of bed at these moments because she feels a heaviness in her

chest that makes it hard to breathe, talk, or do
anything other than sweat profusely. She realizes that
drinking cup after cup of coffee isn't helping her
anxiety, but it seems to be the only way to get through
her day as she navigates between taking care of her
baby and preparing to return to the office. Sara is
desperate to sleep. She is terrified of how she will
adjust to work again, given her difficult, anxious
evenings. She is desperate to get relief from the panic
and some solid sleep.

Can you relate to Sara?

The Need for Good-Quality Sleep

Overcoming and preventing panic and stress requires good-quality sleep. Everyone experiences sleep disruptions, whether they're due to feeling stressed or tending to an infant or family member who needs care in the middle of the night. A few sleep-disrupted nights can be frustrating, but weeks, months, years? In short, ongoing sleep disruption wrecks the balance of your nervous system. Sleep and sleepiness, like respiration, digestion, and heart rate, operate via your vagal nerve and involve your entire immune system. Despite what mattress and supplement companies tell you, if you have a healthy immune system, you have been built to sleep since six months in utero. Sleep is the primary way humans heal and grow. Quality sleep acts as a comfort blanket that repairs, relaxes, and soothes your nervous system, providing feelings of safety and comfort. Sleep deprivation tears that blanket off, exposing you to stress and anxiety. When sleep quality diminishes, your nervous system compensates by leaning on its sympathetic nervous system, pushing adrenaline and cortisol through your bloodstreams to increase energy (Fanselow 2013).

An activated sympathetic nervous system also increases your heart rate, pressure on your digestive tract, sweating, racing thoughts, and many other sensations people describe as panic and anxiety. Like Sara, you may worry so much about your daytime energy that you try to increase it with coffee, energy drinks, or stimulant medications, which can intensify panic symptoms. This cycle is like trying to put out an exploding fireworks finale in your sympathetic nervous system by pouring jet fuel on it.

So what works? How can you get back into consistent quality sleep to help stop and prevent panic and anxiety? Research suggests that engaging your vagus nerve can help readjust your polyvagal system, making it easier to feel tranquil and relaxed, so you can more easily fall asleep and stay asleep through the night (Jiao et al. 2020; Tsai et al. 2015). In other words, if you can find ways to engage the tranquilizing parts of your nervous system, you can help maintain more consistent quality sleep and prevent panic. Stimulating your vagus nerve may sound like it's going to keep you awake, but research has shown that by taking deep, slow breaths, you can improve wakefulness during the day and sleep better at night.

Restoring Quality Sleep

Poor sleep can worsen panic symptoms. Good sleep habits can help you reduce them. While different people need different hours of sleep, aim for at least six hours or more of uninterrupted sleep. Practices and behaviors related to getting better sleep are called *sleep hygiene*. Effective sleep hygiene techniques include:

- creating a daily routine and cooldown space to decompress and shift into sleep

- going to bed only when you're sleepy or have to fight to keep your eyes open

- keeping a consistent daily wake-up time, even on the weekends

- limiting caffeine intake

- sleeping only at night, rather than taking naps or hitting snooze in the morning

- avoiding screens or direct light if you wake up at night

If you're prone to panic, creating a cooldown zone, a space to decompress and shift into sleep, can be particularly helpful in restoring quality sleep. Everyday life requires a lot of calm and focus. Even Marvel Comics' Dr. Stephen Vincent Strange has defended threats to the universe by slipping into relaxed, meditative states. He accomplishes this in his sacred, special place—Sanctum Sanctorum. Every night, you drift into sleep by finding a way to become so relaxed and calm that you can connect to your drive to sleep. When you notice that you fell asleep in a chair or are on a commuter train straining to keep your eyes open, this is due to your sleep drive in action. Your sleep drive flows through your vagus nerve and nervous system. Just like Dr. Strange's Sanctum Santorum helps him focus his powers, a cooldown zone can help you soothe your nervous system and allow your sleep drive to put you to sleep.

Creating a relaxing, easy cooldown zone requires setting some boundaries and enforcing them for about an hour before you go to bed. These include:

- no exposure to screens, including checking emails, texts, or other apps

- no direct light

- no thoughts or conversations about the day or the future

- no clocks or looking at the time

- not going to bed until you're very sleepy or fighting to keep your eyes open

A cooldown zone also requires a separate space from your bed. This can be a comfortable space in the same room as your bed or in a room nearby. Options include a chair, couch, meditation cushion, or pillow.

Sara used a comfy chair near her bed for her cooldown zone. To create a bedtime routine and help her feel sleepy, she replaced screens and clocks with lavender hand lotion and a history podcast. Within a week, Sara could fall asleep and stay asleep for three nights in a row. She felt calmer and less shaky upon waking up.

Create a Cooldown Zone

To create your own cooldown zone, select a comfort-able spot in a room that is protected from outside light when you want to go to bed. If you'd like, add scented essential oils, candles, or lotion that you use only before bed. Pick out a boring podcast or book, which you only listen to or read under low light before going to bed. Plan your wake time.

Follow the same bedtime routine in your cooldown zone for five nights. Get in bed only when you're sleepy enough to fall asleep. Notice any difference in your muscle tension, heart rate, and overall stress each night.

After the fifth day, write a sentence or two about how your stress or body tension has changed since day one. What do you notice? What feels easier or lighter? Review this statement during your cooldown and have it handy if you wake up feeling panicked. Reminding yourself of your progress can help slow your heart rate and induce sleepiness, making it easier to fall back asleep.

If you still feel panicked, instead of staying in bed, move to the cooldown zone and practice relaxing breathing.

Relaxation breathing, also known as four-seven-eight breathing, is an intentional practice of controlled breathing coined by mindfulness pioneer and expert Andrew Weil (1999) to combat anxiety and panic. Research indicates that this kind of controlled breathing stimulates the polyvagal system to induce calm and relaxation in your nervous system (Noble et al. 2019; Tsai et al. 2015).

Try This | Relaxation Breathing

Find a comfortable place outside of your bed to sit or lie on your back. It can be your cooldown zone or some-where else, just not your bed.

Begin by mentally noting how fast your heart is beating, how shallow or tight your breathing feels, and any other muscle pain or tension you might feel, for example, in your back. Once you're settled:

- Count to three while breathing in deeply into your chest.

- Hold your breath for a count of seven.

- Exhale for a count of eight.

If you struggle with respiratory illness or this feels challenging, you can modify to breathing in for three seconds, holding your breath for five seconds, and exhaling for six seconds.

Repeat this breathing pattern ten to twenty times.

Now return your attention to your heart rate, your breath, and your body as a whole. Mentally note: How fast is your heartbeat now? How deep is your breath? Any changes in muscle pain or tension? Write down your observations over a week to track your progress.

Sara finds that creating a cooldown zone, following a bedtime routine consistently, and practicing relaxation breathing allow her to fall asleep and stay asleep. Within a month, she reports no panic symptoms and high satisfaction with her sleep.

When you create a cooldown zone, follow a bedtime routine, and practice relaxation breathing every night, you'll have a much easier time falling asleep and staying asleep consistently.

Takeaways

There are foundational practices, such as establishing good sleep habits, that can protect you from panic and anxiety. Quality sleep restores balance to your nervous system. It also helps you more easily feel safe and confident navigating stressors without falling into panic and anxiety.

When you become sleep deprived, whether it's due to the arrival of a new baby like Sara or simply because you are jetlagged, you lose this safety blanket and can become more easily overwhelmed. Creating daily practices for sleep, like the cooldown zone and relaxation breathing, will help you undo the negative effects of panic and prevent future panic and anxiety. The next chapters offer more foundational practices that stimulate your polyvagal system and allow you respond on the spot to panic and stress and begin restoring balance to your nervous system.

PART 2

Learning to Reregulate When Panic Strikes

CHAPTER 5

Disrupt Panic Sensations

Teaching hundreds of first-year counselors over the years, I have heard the same question come up consistently: how do you help someone stop a panic attack? The question makes sense. Most people I work with who struggle with panic and anxiety report that stopping the intensity of a panic or anxiety attack is the main reason they start psychotherapy.

When I was a medical student studying at university counseling centers in New York City, I felt perpetually frustrated with the limited evidence-based options for treating panic. My training was only in cognitive behavioral therapy (CBT) exposure and prevention and basic mindfulness practices. (CBT is a type of therapy that focuses on changing thoughts and behaviors to treat mental health conditions. We'll talk about mindfulness in chapter 10.) Many patients reported that these interventions could be helpful, but they did not work to stop a panic attack once it started or reduce its intensity. Since then, neuroscience advances have greatly expanded treatment options for people experiencing panic attacks.

Once I understood that panic was a malfunction of the nervous system, like a virus corrupting a computer operating system, it became much easier for me to see panic attacks like computer crashes that require a system reset. Just like the spinning wheel of death on a Mac or the dreaded "program not responding" text flashing in front of a frozen screen, sometimes the nervous system gets overwhelmed to the point that it needs a hard reboot. If you've ever unplugged a frozen computer or dead router and then plugged it back in to restart it, then you've conducted a hard reboot. Hard rebooting your nervous system often requires practices that create intense feelings and safe discomfort, such as exposure to cold temperatures.

★ Rashida's Hard Reboot

Rashida is so tired. She doesn't remember when she had her first panic attack, but she can't recall ever not having them. While working from home during the

COVID lockdown, she notices much more stress and anxiety around her finances and safety. Rashida, an insurance underwriter, is having panic attacks multiple times a day. She is exhausted from the symptoms' intensity and frequency—the pins and needles on the back of her neck, the creeping sense of dread, her racing heart, and a blur of scary thoughts that she's losing her mind. For help, Rashida finally reaches out to a licensed therapist.

In the middle of her first session, Rashida is having a panic attack and has no idea that she will be able to stop it within five minutes by rebooting her nervous system. Rashida begins talking about the dread, and she notices her heart won't stop racing. Her therapist sees that Rashida is slipping into fight-or-flight mode. As we discussed earlier, the highway from the brain to the body runs two ways. Because of this brain-body connection, there are hacks you can do to short out and hard reboot your nervous system when you're having a panic attack.

Rashida learns to hard reboot her system in that first session while she's having a panic attack by using the natural diving response. The natural diving response happens when your head is submerged in water. It forces the opposite of a panic attack to *happen in your nervous system. Breathing slows, the heart rate decreases, and blood flow increases to your brain and heart and away from your arms, legs, and torso. Rashida listens to her therapist, fills a sink with ice and cold water, and then submerges her head. When she comes up out of the sink a moment later, she is amazed. Her panic attack is gone. She feels fatigue and wobbliness but no more discomfort or dread. Suddenly, she can find her words again and begins to share how powerful she feels with this new intervention. Rashida used the ice-submerge method to hard reboot her nervous system.*

Have you felt like Rashida? Stuck in panic and anxiety sensations, looking for some way to stop the discomfort on the spot? One option is to use the sensitivity of your nervous system to overwhelm and reboot yourself out of panic and back into control. When your nervous system detects something uncomfortable, it always pays attention and evaluates whether the source is a real threat.

Luckily, you can take advantage of this vigilance to distract the nervous system. Specifically, research shows that cold exposure can restore calm to your nervous system (Richer et al. 2022). Here are three exercises that use safe exposure to cold temperatures to hard reboot the nervous system.

Ice-Submerge Hard Reboot

Here's an exercise to help you engage your diving response to short out a panic attack and hard reboot your nervous system. When you notice your heart start to race, sweaty palms, feelings of dread, or any other panic symptom begin, try doing the following:

- Fill a sink or tub with ice cubes and water.

- Once the sink is full, submerge your whole head underwater.

- While underwater, close your eyes and hold your breath for ten to fifteen seconds.

- Slowly remove your head from the water.

- Begin breathing by taking four deep inhales and exhales.

It's normal to feel dizzy, wobbly, or fatigued afterward. It's also normal if you still feel ripples of adrenaline and panic. You just stopped a tsunami of adrenaline from spreading through your body, and that takes a lot of energy. Find a comfortable place to rest seated or lying down. If you notice any more dread, repeat the process.

Cold-Shower Hard Reboot

When you notice sweaty palms, shallow and fast breathing, or intense dread that you are about to panic, find a nearby shower. (I once had a client who was mid panic attack when he realized his gym was nearby and jumped into a shower there to do this exercise.)

- Find a shower and run the water until it is lukewarm.

- Gradually turn the temperature of the water down until it feels very cold to hold your hand under it. This is relative to each person, so start with lukewarm and work backward.

- Disrobe fully and get into the cold shower quickly.

- Keep your whole body in the shower for thirty to sixty seconds, or until you notice all that you can pay attention to is how cold you feel.

- Turn off the shower, get out, and wrap yourself in a dry towel.

- Find a comfortable place to rest before getting dressed.

Notice what happens to your panic attack symptoms. It's normal to feel dizzy, wobbly, or fatigued. You just shorted out a giant electrical storm of panic. Rest as long as you need to.

Ice Cube Squeeze

If you notice racing thoughts, worries about an imminent panic attack, or tingly feelings spreading from your chest to your arms and legs, locate an ice cube and do the following:

- Squeeze a single ice cube as hard as you can in one hand. Hold it as long as you can at that intensity. Notice any numbing discomfort you feel in your hand.

- When it feels unbearable to keep squeezing the ice cube, move it to the other hand and repeat.

- Keep switching hands until the ice cube is nearly melted or you notice slower breathing, fatigue, or warmth returning to your body.

If you feel dizzy or disoriented, it's probably because you just shorted out a lot of anxiety and stress from your nervous system and are starting to reboot. Rest as needed.

After practicing any of these three reboot exercises, ask yourself:

- What feels different in my body now compared to before I started?

- What is surprising about this?

- What is relieving about this?

Takeaways

Panic attacks can make you feel helpless, but thanks to your complex and adaptive nervous system, you can short them out with a hard reboot. The natural diving response forces the opposite of a panic attack to happen in your nervous system. Controlled exposure to cold can also reboot your nervous system.

The exercises in this chapter all can be done mid panic attack, should you feel like you are becoming overwhelmed. With a little bit of ice and a lot of neuroscience, you can hard reboot your nervous system and stop panic.

CHAPTER 6

Reset Your Nervous System

Hands sweating. Heart beating out of your chest. Stomach churning. Eyes darting around looking for unseen threats. Any minute, it feels like a dam full of anxiety will burst and drown you in it. This is the buildup of a panic attack that crashes your nervous system, like a computer operating system virus.

When your heart rate picks up, you feel that first wave of pins and needles with cold sweat, or you feel other physical sensations of panic or anxiety, your nervous system is telling you it is distressed. Your nervous system operates like a computer processor that's being highjacked by a malicious app. Like your computer operating system, your nervous system can be rescued from a full crash by engaging other parts of your brain.

Your Brain Has Limited Processing Power

Your brain has only so much processing energy and bandwidth. When your brain is overwhelmed, for example, when you have a panic attack, it can short out. Sensory information that tells your brain you might be in danger forces your brain to divert all its processing resources to survival mode. That doesn't mean you're stuck there though. Just like you used cold exposure in the last chapter's exercises to do a hard reset on your nervous system, there are ways to redirect your brain's focus.

One way to do this is to perform complex cognitive tasks that engage your brain's creative and strategic centers. These types of tasks force your nervous system to redirect brain processing energy away from the places that create panic sensations. This redirection can prevent or stop a panic attack.

Max, a parent of two, spent years in therapy coming to terms with their gender and sexuality, before

*coming out as gay and divorcing their husband. They
also learned to embrace their nonbinary identity,
feeling comfortable using the pronouns they/them for
the past couple years. While they are excited to finally
date in the way they always yearned for, they notice a
problem with panic. On apps and before dates, the
butterflies in their stomach turn quickly into intense
sweating, nausea, and dizziness. Once this starts, they
can't seem to shake it off, resulting in cancelled dates
for fear of embarrassing themself. No matter what
they try, they can't stop thinking about how many
people, like potential dates, will notice the sweat
pouring out of them and run the other way. Feeling
helpless to this cycle, Max decides they might give up
on dating altogether.*

Maybe you've been in Max's shoes, cancelling dates,
work meetings, or other important events because you
can't stop focusing on your panic sensations. In turn, this
focus amps up the symptoms. Let's look at how you can
interrupt this vicious panic cycle by forcing your brain and
nervous system to redirect their attention.

Effects of Complex Cognitive Tasks

Don't believe what your parents told you. Some video-games can be good for you and your brain. Complex puzzle games, like Tetris, Wordle, Sudoku, and crossword puzzles, can prevent panic symptoms by redirecting focus from the brain's emotional centers and into the brain's strategic and creative centers of your brain (the prefrontal cortex and the visual-spatial cortex). MRI studies show that complex visual tasks tax and rewire your brain for increased efficiency, emotional regulation, and learning (Agren et al. 2021; Butler et al. 2020). This is your brain on Candy Crush.

Taking this to heart, Max prepares for their next date by diving into a round of Tetris when they notice their heart rate pick up and the sweat starting on the back of their neck. They feel their heart rate slowing and a cooling sensation around their whole body as they play. They finally stop thinking so much about their panic and go on the date. It's exceptional. It becomes one of the happiest memories in their life.

Let's explore how you can do this too. The following two exercise can help you short out panic by engaging different parts of your brain.

Game Out

Tetris, Sudoku, crosswords, word search, Rubix cube—all of these games require sustained attention and processing in different parts of your brain. This takes your attention and energy away from the parts of your nervous system that fuel panic. For this exercise, follow these steps:

- Acquire one of these games or a similarly cognitively challenging one.

- Think of any activities that cause panic symptoms and notice what happens when you think of them. Maybe thinking of speaking in front of clients makes your heart race? Maybe anticipating an upcoming flight causes your stomach to churn?

- Once you notice any uncomfortable panic or anxiety symptoms starting (such as sweating, increased heart rate, stomach churning, or nausea), set an alarm for five minutes and start playing the cognitive game you have chosen. Focus on playing the game. It doesn't matter how well you do. Just try to keep focusing your attention on the game.

- When the alarm goes off, stop playing.

Ask yourself:

- What feels different in my body now compared to before I started?

- What feels different about my thoughts?

- What is surprising about this?

- What is relieving about this?

- What's still scary about the task or event I was worried about?

Learning to redirect your brain and attention can help you better respond to anxiety and panic in the moment. Practicing a game that requires mental focus daily will strengthen your prefrontal cortex, making it much more efficient and able to readily shift away from the places where panic, anxiety, and dread reside in your nervous system.

Similar to puzzle games like Tetris, drawing, sketching, and doodling force your brain to engage its visual, spatial, and creative areas, which pulls attention and processing away from other areas. You can use these complex visual-spatial tasks to calm, refocus, and restore your mind and body when they get overwhelmed.

Doodle It Out

Have a pad of paper and colored pencils, pens, or markers handy. Don't overthink the materials—you don't need the best pad or dozens of colors.

The next time you notice panic symptoms starting, set a timer for ten minutes and begin drawing or doodling. Focus on just the act of drawing, rather than on how good your drawing is. Remind yourself that no one else will ever see it unless you want them to. You are sketching to short out panic not to get into the Museum of Modern Art.

When the alarm goes off, stop drawing and ask yourself:

- What feels different in my body now compared to before I started?

- What feels different about my thoughts?

- What does this tell me about my worry and panic?

- What is relieving about this?

Practicing this doodling exercise before big meetings or other events that commonly trigger panic sensations can lead to increased mental flexibility and resilience to stress. If you practice this regularly (daily for two months), you will notice a much easier ability to not pay attention to panic symptoms, like nausea, sweating, or intense dread. Some people report no longer having any panic symptoms before public speaking or flying after practicing this for a year or more. So doodle and then give that speech. Color a bit and then get on that flight. The more you practice, the easier it will become to short out panic before it even begins.

Takeaways

Using the exercises in this chapter, you will find that shorting out panic can be fun, creative, and playful. It can be very easy to take panic symptoms too seriously when your brain's emotional and survival centers are regularly engaged. Using complex, stimulating cognitive games and creative activities, like doodling, drawing, or coloring, can help you overcome the heaviness of panic by redirecting your brain's attention. When you practice these skills regularly in response to panic sensations, your nervous system becomes more flexible, efficient, and creative in whatever context you might find yourself, whether it's a first date or a big work presentation.

CHAPTER 7

Learn to Ride the Wave

Since the onset of COVID, Nikhil, a chief resident at a busy hospital, tries daily to white-knuckle through a racing heart and sweating. He's proud of his toughness, but now he feels weak. Ever since he had to start teaching students in the last year, he feels like he hasn't been able to take a deep breath. Some days he can't catch his breath for hours. After a bad night's sleep, he shakes and trembles as pins and needles run up and down his spine. Some days, he stays home from work, worried and embarrassed that others will see him this way.

Have you felt like Nikhil, trying to white-knuckle or push away panic sensations only to find they come back stronger a few moments later? How often have you worried and struggled through intense, painful sensations, like shaking, sweating, or not being able to catch your breath for what feels like hours?

When panic strikes, it can feel like there's a fire exploding inside of you. Neurologically, you're correct. Panic sends supercharged bolts of electricity up and down your nervous system, which inflame everything in their path like a raging wildfire. When your lungs constrict your breathing, when your heart beats harder and faster to move oxygen, and when your stomach starts churning, it can feel like the fires won't ever stop burning. It can seem like these sensations will last forever.

What if I told you all of these sensations happen in minutes, sometimes seconds, and then pass through and out of your nervous system? That's what can happen if you let them do this. What many people never learn is that intense panic sensations are often short, come in waves, and pass over time. Panic and anxiety sensations subside as they travel through your nervous system and vagus nerve. You can turn potential hours of suffering into mere minutes—if you can accept this. Let's explore how you can learn to let panic sensations pass through your nervous system like waves on an ocean.

Accepting sounds easy enough. Yet, one of the most common mistakes people make is trying to use toughness to resist or white-knuckle through panic. When panic strikes, the best thing you can do is find ways to let the painful and uncomfortable sensations pass through you with the least amount of stress—learn to ride the waves of discomfort until they pass.

You don't have to go to Australia's Gold Coast or Hawaii's North Shore to learn how to surf on waves of panic and anxiety without falling under.

Nikhil spends his day off watching online videos, learning from leading researchers about tolerating panic and the waves of discomfort they cause. He stops trying to control his panic sensations and instead rides out each wave of stress, surfing just above the sensations. After a few months of this practice, he is able to within seconds move past shaking and deepen his breathing.

How can you learn to surf waves of panic like Nikhil? Here are some exercises to become a pro at surfing above your anxiety and panic sensations.

Surf the Wave

Surf the wave is an exercise that helps you tolerate distressing panic sensations by imagining your emotions as waves on an ocean. Intense feelings like panic are strong, big waves you can ride like a surfboard. The key to surfing panic symptoms is always knowing that they are temporary and will pass.

Over the next week, when you notice any uncomfortable panic or anxiety symptoms (such as sweating, increased heart rate, stomach churning, or nausea) starting, take a moment to label the feeling. You can avoid judging your feeling by nonjudgmentally asking yourself: What do I feel in this moment? How intense is this feeling right now?

Next, set a timer for three to five minutes and close your eyes. Observe without judgment your feelings and sensations as they rise and fall. Visualize each rising and falling sensation as a wave you are riding above on a magical surfboard on which you never lose your balance. Remind yourself the surfboard will keep you afloat, and the waves will settle down eventually. When your mind drifts, redirect it back to the image of the waves and you riding the surfboard.

When the timer goes off, open your eyes and ask yourself:

- What feels different in my body now compared to before I started?

- What feels easier in my body?

- What is surprising about this?

- What is relieving about this?

- What feeling do I want to take with me back into my day?

Learning to surf the waves of panic and anxiety can help you quickly reduce the intensity and duration of uncomfortable sensations. Practicing this daily will optimize your nervous system's ability to quickly move panic signals through and out of your body with less discomfort. It will also likely reduce inflammation and stress throughout your polyvagal system, leading to fewer panic sensations over time.

Deep in the Ocean Visualization

If you're more of a swimmer than a surfer, this exercise is for you.

The next time you notice panic symptoms, set an alarm for five minutes.

Close your eyes and imagine yourself as a massive ocean, too vast to be fully seen.

Now imagine each panic sensation as a strong wave on the surface of yourself, the ocean. For a few moments, notice how choppy and powerful the waves appear on the surface.

Next, move your attention from the surface of the water to five feet below the surface. Observe how the waves feel different below the surface, where it is less choppy. Stay here for a moment.

Slowly, move your attention deeper into the ocean, hundreds of feet below the surface where there are no waves. Notice how it feels deep, deep down in the ocean.

Slowly move your attention back up to the surface, again observing how strong the waves appear, without pushing any sensation away from you. Remind yourself that you are the entire ocean—not just the waves on the surface.

Finally, bring your attention back to the entire ocean, taking a wide view, where you see the waves on top, the slower water underneath, and the stillness hundreds of feet down. Hold your attention on the entire ocean for a moment.

When the alarm goes off, open your eyes and ask yourself:

- What feels different in my body now compared to before I started?

- What feels comfortable and safe?

- What does this tell me about my worry and panic?

Takeaways

By practicing the exercises in this chapter, you will find that panic and anxiety symptoms can pass quickly and with less pain. When your nervous system is engulfed in panic sensations to the point where it feels like your heart might explode if it beats any harder, slowing down and letting panic sensations pass may feel impossible. Using visualizations to surf or ride out waves of panic can help you reduce the intensity of panic by opening up paths for it to quickly exit your nervous system. When you practice these skills regularly in response to panic sensations, your nervous system becomes quicker and more efficient at letting panic quickly pass.

CHAPTER 8

Practice Opposite Action

Zuri feels like she is drowning. After years of hard work, she got her dream job and is a third-year attorney working at a prestigious law firm. But all she can do is notice the room spinning as her heart feels like it might explode out of her chest any minute. A glass of whiskey or a few puffs from a cannabis pen in the evening seem to make everything feel easier, more distant for a few hours. However, she keeps waking up with racing thoughts about messing up at work. Her fears get worse before any meeting, but particularly the weekly staff meeting. Firm partners attend the meeting, and she's expected to contribute ideas and be ready to answer questions. Zuri has no idea how to

break this cycle and worries she will get stuck in panic
or dependent on substances to do well.

How often have you felt like Zuri? Terrified about having panic symptoms at work and reaching for a glass of wine or an edible to numb the discomfort a bit? Millions of people just like you struggle with this pattern of numbing or succumbing to panic symptoms before group interactions, especially more formal meetings. Are you tired of feeling like you have no choice and being stuck in this pattern? Often, taking the opposite action of what you feel pulled to do can be helpful to stop panic and anxiety.

The vagus nerve is a highway deep in your brain that runs through every major region of your body, sending signals and sensations by the microsecond back and forth from your brain to your body. As discussed in chapter 1, 80 percent of the sensations you experience every day travel on the vagus nerve. When you feel thirsty, hungry, hot, cold, or sexually aroused, and even when you drift off to sleep, you are responding unconsciously to billions of these sensations traveling on the nervous system highway. When you are relaxed, your body can more easily keep your mood and anxiety regulated because the highway is clear of traffic and can easily send information back and forth. However, every panic symptom you experience, like shortness of breath, a racing heartbeat, sweating, or nausea, also travels on that highway.

If you've ever played Super Mario Kart, you know the dread of the blue shell. No matter how smoothly your game is going, how many shortcuts you find, how many banana peels you dodge, or how well you navigate Rainbow Road, when a blue shell is dropped, it will cut through all the other traffic on the road and blow up right on top of you. Panic and anxiety symptoms are the blue shells on your unconscious highway, cutting through all other sensations and exploding your nervous system like a big stress bomb. When you are anxious or panicked, your nervous system becomes inflamed, creating more mixed signals, traffic, and confusion on the highway. Your blood flow and breathing become constricted and tight. The lowered blood flow and restricted breathing reduce oxygen in your bloodstream, forcing your heart to pump harder and faster. Stress levels spike with a flood of stress hormones, like cortisol. When panic sensations flood your nervous system, they create a traffic jam in body signals, causing feelings like rapid temperature changes (that is, feeling really hot or cold), breathing difficulties, rising heart rate, and waves of nausea and cold sweat.

Drinking alcohol or using drugs can numb out or disconnect you from these sensations momentarily, because these substances often block receptors for feeling these sensations in your nervous system. While this numbing and disconnection can be initially relieving, it actually inflames your body and nervous system more, creating more intense rebound panic. Many people describe this experience as "hanganxiety," or extra anxiety, sensitivity, and panic sensations they experience the next day, a hangover from trying to numb out sensations. So how do you clear the traffic and traffic accidents from the highway and avoid making things worse with drugs and alcohol?

Using Opposite Actions

You can resolve these panic traffic jams at a neurological level by engaging consciously in the opposite actions of what your nervous system pulls you to do when you panic (Swain et al. 2013; López and Salas 2009). By engaging in opposite actions, you can redirect your nervous system's responses to slow down your heart and breathing rates. These practices act as roadside assistance, clearing stress hormones from your nervous system to restore stable, easy connections throughout the highway of your brain and nervous system.

Zuri learns how to engage in opposite actions before meetings. A few minutes before the weekly staff meeting, she begins to sweat, her mind starts racing, and she notices she feels a bit like she's choking and can't breathe. Instead of trying to avoid or ignore her panic sensations, she closes her eyes and tunes in to her breathing. She forces herself to breathe more slowly and deeply. She works against the sensations signaling her to quicken her breathing by extending her exhales on each breath. After three minutes, she notices her mind has slowed, she has stopped sweating, and she can breathe easily again. No wine necessary. Filled with pride and confidence, Zuri pitches a winning idea, handling questions easily.

What can you do to soothe your nervous system and resolve panic sensations with opposite action? Turning toward panic sensations may seem counterintuitive, but leaning into panic sensations is akin to moving toward a punch in boxing. Often, you prevent damage this way, while moving away or dodging can get you an uppercut sandwich. Below are a couple evidence-based exercises focused on opposite action (Linehan 2014).

Learning to observe your panic and anxiety sensations will make it easier for you to respond with opposite actions and resist trying to numb or move away from sensations. When practiced daily, the following exercise can strengthen your abilities to visualize and regulate anxiety and panic sensations, so they clear more quickly. When practiced for a year or more, you will notice you can automatically adjust your breathing and heart rate in many high-stress situations without having panic sensations that last more than a minute or two.

Try This Practice Opposite Action

For this exercise, all you need is a text app or paper to write notes and a timer. Here are the four steps to observe and respond to panic sensations with opposite action.

1. Close your eyes and briefly check in with your breathing, heartbeat, body temperature, and stomach. Ask yourself: what feels off in my body?

2. In one or two sentences, write out what exactly feels off. Examples include: My breath feels constricted and shallow. I feel like I can't breathe. My heart feels like it is beating out of my chest. I feel too hot. I feel like I'm going to throw up.

3. Set a timer for two minutes. Close your eyes again and visualize the opposite sensations from your sentence. Say your intention aloud to yourself. Examples include: My heart feels so slow and steady. My stomach feels light. My breath is so slow and deep I could fall asleep. My skin feels comfortable and warm like a perfect spring day. Keep visualizing yourself experiencing these sensations until the timer ends.

4. When you are done visualizing, ask yourself:

   - What feels different in my body now compared to before I started?

   - What is surprising about this?

   - What is relieving about this?

   - What makes me proud about how I handled this?

If you are like millions of people, one of the first things you notice when you experience panic or anxiety sensations is feeling like you're choking, are drowning, or can't breathe. It can feel tempting to spiral out as your chest feels heavier and tighter. Instead, try this intentional practice to soothe yourself, like it soothed Zuri before her staff meeting.

Practicing opposite-action breathing before events that trigger panic sensations, like flying, getting your blood drawn, or going on a date, can prevent the temptation to turn away from or numb panic sensations with drugs or alcohol. If you practice opposite-action breathing as you experience a racing heart, shortness of breath, sweating, nausea, or any other panic or anxiety symptom, you will be able to short out panic sensations quickly without needing a drop of whiskey.

Opposite-Action Breathing

Here are the steps to engage in opposite-action breathing to stop panic symptoms, like the sensation of choking or difficulty breathing:

- Set a timer for three minutes and close your eyes.

- Bring your attention to your breath and lungs. After a moment, bring your attention to your mouth. Imagine you have a tiny straw in your mouth.

- Breath in deeply for three to four seconds through your nose and breath out for five to six seconds through your mouth as if you had a small straw in it.

- Repeat this breathing pattern until the time is up.

When the timer ends, ask yourself:

- Where is my breath now compared to before I started? Does it feel easier or harder to breathe? How light or heavy does my chest feel?

- What is relieving about this?

- What is empowering about this?

Takeaways

Using opposition action, you will be able to use the complex thinking parts of your brain (mainly the prefrontal cortex) to restore balance and stop panic sensations by soothing your nervous system. Daily practice of these skills can not only stop but also prevent panic. Over time, continued practice will allow you to readily shift your breathing and attention to reduce or eliminate panic sensations without as much of a conscious effort.

The best way to get there is for you to intentionally set aside times daily to practice opposite-action breathing, even when you aren't experiencing panic sensations, like difficulty breathing. When do you want to schedule your opposite action practice time today?

PART 3

Keep Your Nervous System Calm and Stable

CHAPTER 9

Benefit from Aerobic Activity

You have gotten through some difficult experiences with panic and anxiety. Now you might be wondering: how can you build a solid immunity against panic overwhelming you in the future? In this chapter, you will learn about how consistent aerobic exercise protects and inoculates your nervous system from being overwhelmed with panic and anxiety. When practiced over time, aerobic exercise increases your *vagal tone*. Vagal tone is like a health meter for your nervous system. Preventative practices, like aerobic exercise, found in this and following chapters will help keep your nervous system's health meter full (high vagal tone), reducing inflammation while increasing brain efficiency and resilience to panic and stress (Balzarotti et al. 2017; Stubbs et al. 2017).

Your high-school gym teacher was right. Intense physical activity is good for you. It's especially good for your brain and nervous system. Aerobic exercise frequently shows up in the research as a nondrug intervention for increasing vagal tone and resilience to stress and pain (Bartley, Hay, and Bloch 2013; Sañudo et al. 2015). Most of the mechanics of panic start with irritation and inflammation throughout the vagus nerve highway in your nervous system. Regular physical exercise increases vagal tone and acts as a street cleaning crew for your nervous system, clearing the road to improve the flow of traffic.

Aerobic activity improves blood flow and deepens breathing, stimulating your vagus nerve to reduce irritation, inflation, and stress signals in your body. Practiced over time, aerobic activity acts an inoculation against panic and anxiety sensations by making sure your health meter is full. The evidence for aerobic exercise in protecting people from panic and anxiety continues to mount. In study after study (da Costa et al. 2022; Luo et al. 2022), when people engaged in daily exercise, even during the COVID lockdowns, their anxiety and panic sensations were reduced or eliminated in weeks.

Before Martin's son was born, Martin had a lot of
anxiety about being a caring and attentive parent as
well as being able to provide financially for his family.
His head would spin with racing thoughts, and he
often felt like he couldn't breathe. Eventually, Martin
went to his cardiologist, who referred him to therapy
for anxiety. Working in therapy, he was able to
overcome his anxiety before his son was born. Now
Martin is back at work, balancing his job and
nighttime care for his 6-month-old son. He worries his
panic and anxiety will come back, and he worries
about what he'll do if this happens.

Have you ever worried like Martin? Have you completed therapy or overcome prior panic or anxiety symptoms, then worried these will come back with a new life challenge or stressor?

You can use regular aerobic exercise to pump up your vagal tone and help prevent future panic and anxiety. You don't need a fancy gym or any special equipment or training program. You just need to be able to push yourself to the point of sweating. It might sound gross, but the more you sweat, the more you build up your vagal tone.

Before you start a new exercise regimen, check in with your healthcare provider. Also, if you're used to being sedentary, start small and gradually build up endurance. Walking can be a great option, and you can gradually increase duration and distance over time, before progressing to aerobic activities, such as intervals. Above all, remember that any exercise you do is beneficial! If the exercises described below don't work for you, ask your healthcare provider about other exercise options, such as swimming.

Any amount of aerobic exercise builds vagal tone and improves your nervous system's ability to respond to stress on a neurological level. If you want to up your game, high-intensity interval training (HIIT) optimizes these benefits. Research indicates that while aerobic activity helps relieve panic in the short term, HIIT, like cardiovascular activity circuits, can protect people from panic and anxiety symptoms for years.

Following are some time-efficient exercises that can help protect you from anxiety and panic (towel not included). Starting off training every day, even for a shorter duration, will help you establish an exercise habit. If every day doesn't work for you, aim for three to five times a week—but still put each session on your calendar as a time commitment. Scheduling specific times and/or days also supports making exercise a habit.

Brace yourself. It's about to get sweaty.

High-Intensity Interval Training

In your calendar, block off fifteen to twenty minutes every day for the next week for HIIT.

If you have access to an exercise bike, treadmill, or elliptical machine, adjust settings to a light resistance that you can maintain without sweating or breathing heavily. You can also use a jump rope or go outside for a walk, jog, or bike ride.

For an HIIT session:

- Start with one minute of easy exercise.

- After one minute, increase your pace or resistance for one minute. Push yourself to the point of sweating and breathing heavily.

- Continue to alternate one minute of easy exercise with one minute of faster or harder exercise.

- Work up to repeating this two-minute pattern eight to ten times.

Remember that you may need to build up your endurance gradually to get to a full twenty minutes each session. Hang in there. It does get easier.

Once you have completed a workout, ask yourself:

- What feels comfortable in this moment?

- What feels strong in this moment?

- What feels clear in this moment?

Martin discovers his anxiety and worry disappear after doing a brief high-intensity aerobic workout at his gym. The next day, he helps his wife move some furniture up and down stairs until he is sweaty and out of breath, and again his worries mysteriously disappear. Martin decides to commit to twenty minutes of sweating and heavy breathing daily. By his son's first birthday, he can't remember what he was so worried about.

What if you could stay this calm? What if you could ensure resilience to panic and stress by maintaining this practice?

Destress Stairs

If high-intensity cardio is too challenging for you, don't worry, you have other options. This exercise, which will increase your vagal tone to build resilience to panic and stress, requires access to stairs and fifteen minutes.

Find a time in your calendar where you can block off fifteen minutes daily for the next week and schedule destress stairs. Locate a set of stairs nearby where you won't be disturbed.

When the time comes for exercise, set a timer for fifteen minutes and walk up and down the stairs until the timer ends. You should be sweaty and have difficulty talking, due to being out of breath, by eight minutes. If you notice that you aren't feeling this way, increase your pace and continue.

Keep in mind that, depending on your fitness level and agility when you start, it can take weeks or even months to build up to fifteen minutes of stair climbing. Do the best you can. Give yourself props for adding any physical activity. Rest or stop at any point if you feel too winded or tired.

When the timer ends, stop walking and ask yourself:

- What feels comfortable in this moment?

- What feels strong in this moment?

- What feels clear in this moment?

Takeaways

Using the exercises in this chapter, you will develop a foundation for making your nervous system resilient to panic and anxiety. Practicing high-intensity interval training or destress stairs rewires your brain to better handle stress and anxiety. Practiced consistently over years, aerobic exercise reduces overall inflammation in your entire body, protecting you not only from anxiety and panic but also from health conditions such as heart and lung disease. The more frequently and consistently you exercise, the more benefit you'll see. Any exercise is beneficial, so do what works best for you and give yourself credit for making this commitment to your health. But who knew a healthy, panic-free life would be this sweaty?

CHAPTER 10

Practice Mindfulness

The benefits of mindfulness are numerous. Mindfulness practice keeps your nervous system resilient and protected from panic and anxiety. With consistent practice, mindfulness reduces stress and inflammation in your nervous system by stimulating your vagus nerve to release antiinflammatory, calming signals throughout your brain and body. By increasing your vagal tone, mindfulness protects and prevents panic from disrupting your heart rate, breathing, and digestion. Mindfulness practice creates a sense of safety by steadying your heartbeat, inducing deeper breathing, and slowing down thinking. The benefits of mindfulness include making it easier for you to interact well with others, even when you're stressed or overwhelmed.

What Is Mindfulness?

Mindfulness is directing your conscious attention and senses (seeing, hearing, smelling, touching, tasting) to the present moment without judging or trying to make sense of it. When thoughts or feelings distract you (and they will), you simply acknowledge them and return your focus to the present. If you have ever slowed down to savor the last bites of a cheesecake, you have practiced mindfulness. Research using brain scans shows that mindfulness practice alters the brain's stress response, making it more efficient in handling problems, stress, and anxiety (Creswell et al. 2016).

With consistent mindfulness practice, your brain becomes much more flexible and open, making learning, connecting to others, and solving complex problems easier. Overall, mindfulness optimizes your nervous system, making life calmer and more satisfying.

Mindfulness practice creates new antianxiety circuits in your nervous system, which help prevent and protect against panic and anxiety. The most elite operators and leadership in the military understand this. Navy SEALS make mindfulness practice a core of their training. Through months of mindfulness practice, SEALs rewire their brains, learning how to keep their heart rate and breathing steady and calm, whether or not a mine is exploding next to their heads.

When your job regularly requires you to think clearly and quickly while bullets and explosives rain down around you, it's understandable that you need effective defenses against panic and anxiety.

Lisa, a veteran and small business owner, knows what it feels like to stay calm in a war zone. She served a combat tour in Afghanistan when she was nineteen and never seemed to lose her nerve or get flustered driving through open gunfire at high speed. Recently, though, Lisa got into a minor car accident and hasn't been able to drive more than a mile without worrying about losing her calm and becoming lightheaded.

Lisa feels embarrassed and weak given what she was able to do in the military. She seeks out a workshop at a veterans' wellness conference, where she learns mindfulness practices from a military psychologist, who's also a Navy SEAL. She adopts these practices and begins doing them before each drive. Within a few weeks, Lisa notices feeling stronger and calmer, no longer worrying about driving and even planning out a cross-country road trip for her family.

How often have you wanted to feel strong and calm when faced with panic and anxiety? Don't enlist just yet. You don't need to be in the military to learn mindfulness practices that will keep you resilient and protected from panic.

Following are two of the mindfulness exercises Lisa learned, which build neurological resilience to panic and anxiety. The first exercise, tactical breathing, also known as tactical combat breathing, is a mindfulness practice the military developed that is designed to increase calm and reduce anxiety in any situation.

Try This · Tactical Breathing

Find a time daily when you have five minutes to practice, for example, before or after a meal. Schedule it in your calendar for the next week.

When it's time to practice, settle yourself in a comfortable position. This is a do-anywhere exercise, so sit, lie down, or stand.

Close your eyes and bring your attention to your breath and lungs.

Focus on your breath without changing it for five to ten breaths. When your mind wanders (and it will), bring your attention gently back to your breath.

Next, set an alarm for four minutes. Again, close your eyes and focus on your breath. Instead of just observing, consciously alter your breath and follow this pattern:

- Breathe in while counting "one, two, three, four."

- Stop. Hold your breath while counting "one, two, three, four."

- Exhale while counting "one, two, three, four."

Continue to repeat this pattern, focusing on counting and your breath. When your mind wanders, gently bring it back to your breath and the count.

When the alarm goes off, slowly open your eyes and ask yourself:

- What feels different in my body now compared to before I started?

- What feels calming?

- What is surprising about this?

- What is relieving about this?

Next, water-tank visualization is a mindfulness exercise based on mindfulness practices taught to Navy SEALs and other military leaders (Divine 2015). This practice is designed to clear your mind of thoughts or feelings, including anxiety and panic sensations. When you engage in this practice, you stimulate your vagus nerve, releasing a cascade of calming and relaxing signals in your body.

Try This — Water-Tank Visualization

Find a time daily when you can practice this exercise for five minutes. It doesn't matter if it's at the same time every day. Schedule water-tank exercise in your calendar daily for the next week.

Start by setting an alarm for five minutes and taking a few deep breaths. After your second breath, let your eyes close. Bring your attention to your breath, letting it settle naturally. Don't try to change or deepen your breathing. Just notice where it is in this moment.

Imagine you have stepped inside your mind and you find a large murky, water tank in the middle of the space. Light appears to be streaming in through a glass window, shining on the murky water.

Now imagine that as you breathe, each exhale appears to make the water a bit cleaner. With each breath you take, notice how the water becomes clearer, with light starting to shine through the tank's glass window. Each time your mind wanders, the water becomes dirtier, murkier, and harder to see through. However, as you bring your attention back to the tank and your breathing, the water again becomes clear.

Continue breathing, noticing how much clearer the water becomes with each breath. In time, notice that the water is very clear, almost a tropical blue color, which you can see through the window. You can also see the light going right through the clear, blue water.

Keep focusing on the clear, clean water as you continue to breathe.

When your alarm goes off, slowly close the door to your mind, open your eyes, and bring yourself back to the present.

Ask yourself:

- What feels different in my mind now versus before I started the exercise?

- What feels clear?

- What is surprising about this?

- What is comforting about this?

Takeaways

Mindfulness practices in this chapter build strong immunities to future panic and anxiety by stimulating your vagus nerve, increasing vagal tone, and allowing your nervous system to run smoothly and efficiently. If you want to train your nervous system to become as strong and resilient as a Navy SEAL, practice these exercises daily. After a few weeks, you will become much more adept at observing and avoiding anxious sensations and thoughts that lead to panic. After months of daily practice, your vagal tone will be strong enough that you will be able to quickly recalibrate and overcome panic sensations without much conscious thought. After years of practice, your risk of panic, cardiovascular events like heart attacks or strokes, and early death all drop significantly. If you want a long, panic-free life, where can you fit mindfulness practice into every day?

CHAPTER 11

Work with Panic Thoughts

No matter how many times you preview it, you can't seem to stop it. You can see it all in your mind. In fact, it replays daily, like some evil streaming show on a loop in your brain. Your palms sweat. Your heart beats out of your chest in the middle of a big meeting. Everyone sees it. You're humiliated. You can't stop previewing the worst outcomes where your panic always destroys your life. When you preview a future panic attack, your nervous system feels like it's happening and switches into survival mode. Your heart races, your lungs tighten, and all your thoughts seem to speed up. Suddenly only catastrophic outcomes seem inevitable, triggering and inflaming your nervous system with uncomfortable panic sensations. How often have you been stuck in this vicious loop?

Ben, a digital designer, lost his grandmother during the first wave of COVID in 2020. Terrified by thoughts about dying on a respirator or in his sleep, he had a panic attack that same year, leading him to further isolate from others. Ben has avoided going out for the last few years. He has been able to accelerate his career while working remotely. Now he has a new promotion opportunity as an art director that requires regular travel to conferences and events.

Ben can think about only the worst-case scenario. He imagines having panic attacks at work and begins to get flashes of hot, sharp, uncomfortable pins and needles on his back. Suddenly, he can't stop thinking about getting sick and dying during the course of his new job. Ben keeps himself up for a few nights worrying about his career and what panic might do to derail it.

Have you ever felt as powerless as Ben? What can you do to protect yourself from catastrophic thinking and the panic it creates?

Your Very Own Spider-Sense

In the Marvel comic *Spider-Man*, Peter Parker finds himself gifted with an impressive assortment of superpowers from a radioactive-spider bite. While he can crawl on walls and shoot spiderweb threads, his most impressive power is his spider-sense. Extending from his unconscious brain, Spider-Man's spider-sense quickly sends signals from his environment directly to his conscious system. Thanks to his spider-sense, Spider-Man can quickly sense danger, dodge threats, and respond effectively, whether the situation is a cat in a tree or the villainous Green Goblin.

Cognitive restructuring is the brain's form of spider-sense for responding to thoughts about panic and anxiety—so they don't turn into panic attacks and anxiety. *Cognitive restructuring* is a power provided by the prefrontal cortex that allows your nervous system to keep you calm and focused even when faced with scary thoughts or threatening environments—no radioactive spiders necessary. When you utilize cognitive restructuring, you can quickly swap out catastrophic, distorted thoughts for more realistic, helpful thoughts (Shurick et al. 2012). Over time, engaging your cognitive-restructuring abilities increases your immunity to future panic and anxiety, allowing you to become more adept at quick, logical decision-making. Just like Spider-Man had to learn to use his superpowers, you can learn how to use cognitive restructuring.

When faced with scary thoughts and predictions, your brain will always seek out the biggest and most threatening predictions first. Focusing on the worst-case scenario or predictions is your brain's way of trying to protect you from the biggest threats. The problem is that all of these threats are made-up thoughts. These fantasy nightmare predictions are not real, but they can feel real and threatening if you remain stuck on them. A common mistake people make is focusing only on their worst-case predictions and most catastrophic thoughts about the future. If you can instead consciously rewrite your catastrophic thoughts and predictions, you can engage your cognitive restructuring to prevent panic and anxiety from overwhelming your nervous system.

Desperate for some help, Ben attends an online workshop about cognitive restructuring run by a psychologist. In the course, he learns practices to reduce his fixation on the worst-case scenario, where he melts down and can't function due to panic at his new job. He learns to change his internal narratives, rewiring his brain so it can remain calm when considering his new job. After practicing cognitive-restructuring exercises for a few days, Ben is able to clearly preview his future without panic and dread. He excitedly accepts the new job, repeating the exercises daily and staying panic free at his new job. Within a year, he is promoted again and can't remember why he was so stuck on catastrophic thoughts before.

The following exercises will help you engage and strengthen your cognitive-restructuring abilities. They help prevent panic attacks by rewiring your nervous system to respond optimally, no matter how scary your thoughts or predictions become.

Rewrite Predictions

You can do the writing part of this exercise on paper or using a text app. You will also need an app that can record you speaking out loud. Here are the steps to rewrite predictions:

DESCRIBE THE WORST-CASE SCENARIO. In a few sentences, write out your current scariest prediction about what panic or anxiety will do to you in the future. Are you unable to catch your breath and completely blow a big speech? Do you lose your job? Are you homeless? How big and bad does your prediction get? Whatever it is, write it down and label it "worst-case scenario."

DESCRIBE THE BEST-CASE SCENARIO. Now, in a few sentences, do the opposite by writing out a positive prediction about what panic and anxiety will do to you in the future. This scenario should be just as extreme as your worst case. Don't worry about making it realistic. Make it the best outcome for you possible. Does your panic magically disappear? It never comes back ever, and every part of your life becomes better? How good does it get? Label this description "best-case scenario."

DESCRIBE REALISTIC PREDICTIONS AND THOUGHTS. Think of three or four predictions and outcomes that include both good and bad experiences, but that aren't the worst or best case. Ben writes out a few scenarios where he has panic or gets COVID but is able to do well at his job or doesn't get hospitalized. Write a few sentences for each prediction. Label these "realistic predictions and thoughts."

RECORD REALISTIC PREDICTIONS AND THOUGHTS. Read each of these realistic predictions and thoughts out loud to yourself. Then choose the two realistic predictions and thoughts that feel the most comforting and calming. Open a voice-recorder app and record yourself reading both predictions aloud. Save this file as "realistic predictions and thoughts" with the date.

THINK ABOUT THE EFFECTS OF THE EXERCISE. After completing the recording, ask yourself:

- What feels different in my body now compared to before I started?

- What thoughts feel easier to reflect on?

- What is surprising about this?

- What is relieving about this?

For the next few weeks, try practicing the rewrite predictions exercise daily. Don't worry about repeating yourself. You may notice the same or similar thought patterns and predictions come up. This is common and likely means you have found a specific neural path that you will rewire over time. Brain-imaging research indicates that regular practice over weeks and months changes your brain, so it more efficiently engages cognitive restructuring. When practiced daily for a year or more, your brain becomes much more resilient to fear and panic, while improving decision-making and emotional regulation across your nervous system.

After a few weeks of engaging in the rewriting your predictions practice, you will have a folder full of realistic predictions recordings. You can use these to strengthen and reinforce new neural paths against panic as both a practice and an intervention tool.

As a practice tool, listen to your realistic predictions two or three times a week. This enables you to rehearse different thinking patterns. By doing so, you can create a kind of muscle memory for your nervous system to use when faced with new stressors, so it can more quickly connect to helpful, realistic, and calming thoughts and predictions. The following exercise explains how to use these recordings as an intervention tool when you notice that your mind starts to focus or fixate on worst-case outcomes.

Use Your Rewritten Predictions

If you find yourself fixated on worst-case outcomes, open your files of realistic predictions and thoughts and play them on a repeating loop.

Next, set an alarm for two minutes.

Close your eyes and listen to the recordings. When other thoughts come into your mind, direct your attention back to listening.

When the alarm ends, stop playing the recordings.

Open your eyes and ask yourself the following questions:

- What thoughts feel clearer compared to before you listened to the recordings?

- What tasks or activities feel easier?

- What is surprising about this?

- What is relieving about this?

Takeaways

Practicing the exercises in this chapter will strengthen your cognitive-restructuring abilities. These skills help prevent catastrophic thoughts and panic sensations. You can also use them an intervention tool if you find yourself fixating on worst-case outcomes. Daily practice over years will change the wiring of your brain, making your nervous system better able to keep you calm when faced with stress. Research indicates that over time, cognitive-restructuring practices thicken your brain's circuits, changing how your brain engages fear. This decreases the risk of panic and anxiety overwhelming your nervous system. You may not be a superhero, but stronger cognitive-restructuring abilities will give you a new power to face panic.

CHAPTER 12

Coregulate to Keep Yourself on Track

Panic and anxiety can feel isolating. How often have you felt alone in your most panicked moments? How often have you found yourself physically isolated when your mind races, your heart speeds up with adrenaline, or waves of cold rush up your spine? Panic and anxiety make you feel unsafe and threatened, switching you into survival mode. In survival mode, every kitten appears to be a saber-toothed tiger, and every human is a potential assailant.

Panic doesn't just feel isolating. It is isolating. To help prevent panic and cope with it when it happens, connecting to other people is not just helpful but essential.

Forget what Descartes said. What makes you human is not "I think therefore I am," but instead "I connect therefore I am." We have evolved from thousands of years of human interactions and culture all leading to the same conclusion: we are fully able to function well only when we are connected to other people. This premise is at the heart of polyvagal theory and key to protecting you from panic and anxiety. When you feel safe, you can build these connections by reaching out to others, even when you feel overwhelmed and alone. In fact, that's an especially important time to reach out.

When you feel safe and connected to others, the risk of overwhelming panic and anxiety decreases. Humans have evolved socially. Our bodies and minds are built to be socially engaged. One of your superpowers is coregulation, the ability to affect and soothe strong, difficult emotions and sensations in other humans. You observe and experience coregulation every day but probably never notice it. When a parent soothes a crying baby, when a person gives directions to a lost person, even when you give a hug to your partner after a bad day, people use coregulation to soothe each other. Over thousands of years, humans have learned to do this well. We've overcome individual fears and anxieties of being eaten by saber-toothed tigers or dying of starvation to collectively build tools, invent farming, and grow entire civilizations.

The superheroes Guardians of the Galaxy have a lot to teach us about the power of coregulation. Through multiple destructions of the universe, the Guardians have stayed standing thanks to the team's strong connections. Building close, intimate bonds, the team is able to help each other feel safe and supported, even in the direst situations. How do they do this? Through coregulation, they have changed each other's brains.

Coregulation, which requires connections with other people, makes the brain more efficient and resilient to stress. Across neurological studies (Kok et al. 2013), people who connect socially with others to share feelings and problems have higher vagal tone, higher stress resilience, and lower anxiety and panic. When faced with terrifying opponents and huge spikes of panic and anxiety, the Guardians coregulate by making space to talk it out and figure out their pain and problems together. Every time Star-Lord or Rocket Racoon opens up to each other, shows some compassion, or shares a laugh during a tense moment, they improve the functioning of their brains on a neurological level. While the Guardians have many impressive individual talents and powers, as a team, they have survived the hardest times through coregulation.

Do you have a group of friends you turn to like Guardians? Who is your Rocket Racoon and Groot? Who are the people you turn to for support and validation when you struggle with panic and anxiety? Here's a practice you can do to prevent future panic by fostering coregulation in your life.

Try This

Coregulation Conversation

Think of a friend who has been helpful and friendly to you. It doesn't matter if you have spoken to this friend before about your thoughts or feelings, just that you trust them and feel safe around them.

Reach out to this friend and make plans to meet up for an activity where you will be able to talk and listen face-to-face for ten minutes. Don't overthink this. Grab a coffee or go for a walk in the park. The activity doesn't matter as long as you can hear each other.

When you meet up, ask your friend if you can share something hard about your life. Share one thing you are having a hard time with or worrying about. Be as honest and open as you feel comfortable. Ask them to refrain from giving you advice. Instead, tell them it feels very good to be listened to. Don't overthink the share. If you're worried it will be too much for you or your friend, share a minor worry or frustration. What matters is that you practice honestly sharing a concern aloud to a person you trust.

After your friend listens, thank them for taking the time to listen and offer to do the same for them. Ask them if they are having a hard time with anything and want someone like you to listen to them without advice. Don't worry if they don't want to share. The practice works whether they share with you or not. However, many people enjoy sharing in this way because it provides comfort and safety through coregulation, so don't be surprised if they take you up on your offer.

After meeting with your friend and having a coregulation conversation, ask yourself the following questions:

- How alone or isolated do I feel compared to before I met with my friend?

- How close do I feel to my friends and family? To this friend specifically?

- What does my body feel like?

- What is comforting about this?

- What is relieving about this?

You can deepen your connections and make coregulation a constant in your life by scheduling weekly hangouts and meetups with different friends to practice the coregulation conversation. When practiced weekly over months, you will notice reduced panic sensations and increased feelings of safety and connection. You will also notice increases in empathy, emotional intelligence, self-compassion, and optimism. Practiced over years, coregulation conversations rewire your reactions to emotions such as panic and anxiety.

Seeking Professional Help

What if you don't have anyone in your life to turn to for support? What if you have friends and family, but your panic sensations are still overwhelming?

While coregulation and the other exercises in this book can be helpful for panic and anxiety, they might not be enough. If you are having panic attacks to the point where they persistently disrupt your relationships, work, and/or satisfaction in life, consider seeking professional therapy. Mental health therapy by a licensed provider is the most effective treatment for panic and anxiety. This likely is not news to you, but you may still wonder about the best way to find good therapy.

The emergence of new technologies and options for dealing with panic and anxiety can make it even more daunting to figure out what's the best, most competent, and safest treatment for you. Here are some tips if you're looking to connect to treatment and not sure where do start and what to look for.

- Use websites like Psychology Today or Good Therapy that require a license to register. These websites provide links to and contact info for providers who are licensed to treat mental health disorders. Notice providers who specialize in treating panic and anxiety listed within the first few sentences of their bio or description.

- Reach out to universities that have postgraduate training for therapy and ask for referrals. Many universities have postgraduate training programs or fellowships, where licensed providers can get specialty training in treating anxiety and other disorders. An online search in your state can help you find these programs.

- Avoid apps and online "health/life" coaches. Look for a licensed provider who's available in person or via telehealth. While you can find an endless number of mental health apps (some of which, such as meditation apps, may be helpful) and online coaches, these options are not therapy, nor are they as effective as therapy.

Final Takeaway

Coregulation is a powerful final tool in your toolbox for overcoming panic and anxiety. When you interact with others by practicing coregulation conversations, you are able to call on your polyvagal system to calm you. Practicing coregulation conversations increases your sense of safety and control in the world. If coregulation is helpful but you still struggle with panic and anxiety, therapy might be the best strategy for you. Remember all of the exercises in this book can be a helpful adjunct to clinical treatment.

You made it through the entire book, learning many different ways to strengthen your polyvagal system and overcome anxiety and panic. This is hard work. Millions of people all around the world struggle to escape panic, and many never finding ways to help themselves. Except for you. If you spent even a minute practicing one exercise in this book, you've done more to overcome panic and anxiety than many people ever accomplish—be proud.

You might have found some practices to be helpful, while others weren't. That's perfectly normal. It's not necessary to do every exercise in this book. Instead, I encourage you to keep trying different exercises until you find a few that are consistently helpful. Make those practices a part of your toolbox for overcoming panic and anxiety. If you found anything to take from this book that makes you feel more hopeful and capable of overcoming panic and anxiety, then I am thrilled. I'm proud of how much work you have already put in. Keep your progress going—find your inner Triforce, win the race down Rainbow Road, but remember you're never alone. I'll be cheering for you the entire way!

Acknowledgments

Writing a book takes a lot of people. I am forever indebted to my parents, who taught me to love writing and made me feel proud of each sentence. To my entire family, who kept believing in me from high-school graduation to doctoral convocation.

Thank you, Seth Porges, for giving me your vote of confidence in writing about polyvagal theory from day one. I am in the debt of Steven Porges and Deb Dana, whose work acted as a foundation for this book.

A very special thanks to Jacqueline Mattis, Mary Sue Richardson, Lisa Suzuki, and the entire NYU Counseling Psychology doctorate program, who took a chance, offered me a scholarship, and gave me so much more. As a grandchild of people who somehow walked out of Auschwitz and into New Jersey, I never dreamed I would be a doctor, let alone write a book. My family will always be in your debt.

To Deirdra Frum, the Outpatient DBT Team, and the psychology training team at the Northport VA Medical Center, my deepest gratitude for the hundreds of hours you spent training me in mindfulness-based therapies and DBT. Your encouragement and confidence throughout my internship year made me the psychologist I am today.

I never would have received that scholarship to New York University without the constant support and feedback I have received from Mary Pilon. Mary, thank you for always being in my corner and finding the time to read my work.

Writing about neuroscience so that anyone can understand and use it is not something they teach you in graduate school. I am forever grateful to Fritz Galette for agreeing to make me the research director for his public radio show. You taught me how to make psychology accessible to everyday people and to never lose my sense of humor. I hope you are proud of how much this wisdom is in the book.

I would be totally lost in this entire process without the guidance and support from the entire New Harbinger crew. Thank you for giving me this opportunity to take my knowledge out of the classrooms at NYU and help so many more people struggling with panic and anxiety.

When Panic Happens

Finally, none of this would have been possible without the encouragement and cheerleading of my wife, Erin. Keeping my confidence as a writer has been a struggle, and you have always been there pushing me along and singing my praises to anyone who will listen. I love you. Thank you.

References

Agren, T., J. M. Hoppe, L. Singh, E. A. Holmes, and J. Rosén. 2021. "The Neural Basis of Tetris Gameplay: Implicating the Role of Visuospatial Processing." *Current Psychology* 42: 8136–8163.

Balzarotti, S., F. Biassoni, B. Colombo, and M. R. Ciceri. 2017. "Cardiac Vagal Control as a Marker of Emotion Regulation in Healthy Adults: A Review." *Biological Psychology* 130: 54–66.

Bartley, C. A., M. Hay, and M. H. Bloch. 2013. "Meta-Analysis: Aerobic Exercise for the Treatment of Anxiety Disorders." *Progress in Neuro-Psychopharmacology and Biological Psychiatry* 45: 34–39.

Butler, O., K. Herr, G. Willmund, J. Gallinat, S. Kühn, and P. Zimmermann. 2020. "Trauma, Treatment and Tetris: Video Gaming Increases Hippocampal Volume in Male Patients with Combat-Related Posttraumatic Stress Disorder." *Journal of Psychiatry and Neuroscience* 45(4): 279–287.

Creswell, J. D., A. A. Taren, E. K. Lindsay, C. M. Greco, P. J. Gianaros, A. Fairgrieve, et al. 2016. "Alterations in Resting-State Functional Connectivity Link Mindfulness

Meditation with Reduced Interleukin-6: A Randomized Controlled Trial." *Biological Psychiatry* 80(1): 53–61.

da Costa, T. S., A. Seffrin, J. de Castro Filho, G. Togni, E. Castardeli, C. A. Barbosa de Lira, R. L. Vancini, B. Knechtle, T. Rosemann, and M. S. Andrade. 2022. "Effects of Aerobic and Strength Training on Depression, Anxiety, and Health Self-Perception Levels During the COVID-19 Pandemic." *European Review for Medical and Pharmacological Sciences* 26(15): 5601–5610.

Dana, D. 2020. *Polyvagal Exercises for Safety and Connection: 50 Client-Centered Practices.* New York: W. W. Norton.

Divine, M. 2015. *Unbeatable Mind: Forge Resiliency and Mental Toughness to Succeed at an Elite Level*, 3rd ed. San Diego, CA: US Tactical.

Fanselow, M. S. 2013. "Fear and Anxiety Take a Double Hit from Vagal Nerve Stimulation." *Biological Psychiatry* 73(11): 1043–1044.

Hayes, S. C., K. D. Strosahl, and K. G. Wilson. 2011. *Acceptance and Commitment Therapy: The Process and Practice of Mindful Change.* New York: Guilford Press.

Jiao, Y., X. Guo, M. Luo, S. Li, A. Liu, Y. Zhao, et al. 2020. "Effect of Transcutaneous Vagus Nerve Stimulation at Auricular Concha for Insomnia: A Randomized Clinical Trial." *Evidence-Based Complementary and Alternative Medicine (eCAM)* 2020: 6049891.

Kok, B. E., K. A. Coffey, M. A. Cohn, L. I. Catalino, T. Vacharkulksemsuk, S. B. Algoe, M. Brantley, and B. L. Fredrickson. 2013. "How Positive Emotions Build Physical Health: Perceived Positive Social Connections

Account for the Upward Spiral Between Positive Emotions and Vagal Tone." *Psychological Science* 24(7): 1123–1132.

Linehan, M. 2014. *DBT Skills Training Manual*, 2nd ed. New York: Guilford Press.

López, F. J. C., and S. Valdivia Salas. 2009. "Acceptance and Commitment Therapy (ACT) in the Treatment of Panic Disorder: Some Considerations from the Research on Basic Processes." *International Journal of Psychology and Psychological Therapy* 9(3): 299–315.

Luo, Q., P. Zhang, Y. Liu, X. Ma, and G. Jennings. 2022. "Intervention of Physical Activity for University Students with Anxiety and Depression During the COVID-19 Pandemic Prevention and Control Period: A Systematic Review and Meta-Analysis." *International Journal of Environmental Research and Public Health* 19(22): 15338.

Noble, L. J., A. Chuah, K. K. Callahan, R. R. Souza, and C. K. McIntyre. 2019. "Peripheral Effects of Vagus Nerve Stimulation on Anxiety and Extinction of Conditioned Fear in Rats." *Learning & Memory* 26(7): 245–251.

Porges, S. W. 2011. *The Polyvagal Theory: Neurophysiological Foundations of Emotions, Attachment, Communication, and Self-Regulation*. New York: W. W. Norton.

———. 2022. "Polyvagal Theory: A Science of Safety." *Frontiers in Integrative Neuroscience* 16: 871227.

Porges, S. W., and D. Dana. 2018. *Clinical Applications of the Polyvagal Theory: The Emergence of Polyvagal-Informed Therapies*. New York: W. W. Norton.

Richer, R., J. Zenkner, A. Küderle, N. Rohleder, and B. M. Eskofier. 2022. "Vagus Activation by Cold Face Test

Reduces Acute Psychosocial Stress Responses." *Scientific Reports* 12(1): 19270.

Rosenberg, S. 2017. *Accessing the Healing Power of the Vagus Nerve: Self-Help Exercises for Anxiety, Depression, Trauma, and Autism*. Berkeley, CA: North Atlantic Books.

Sañudo, B., L. Carrasco, M. de Hoyo, A. Figueroa, and J. M. Saxton. 2015. "Vagal Modulation and Symptomatology Following a 6-Month Aerobic Exercise Program for Women with Fibromyalgia." *Clinical and Experimental Rheumatology* 33(1 Suppl 88): S41–S45.

Shurick, A. A., J. R. Hamilton, L. T. Harris, A. K. Roy, J. J. Gross, and E. A. Phelps. 2012. "Durable Effects of Cognitive Restructuring on Conditioned Fear." *Emotion* 12(6): 1393–1397.

Stubbs, B., D. Vancampfort, S. Rosenbaum, J. Firth, T. Cosco, N. Veronese, G. A. Salum, and F. B. Schuch. 2017. "An Examination of the Anxiolytic Effects of Exercise for People with Anxiety and Stress-Related Disorders: A Meta-Analysis." *Psychiatry Research* 249: 102–108.

Swain, J., K. Hancock, C. Hainsworth, and J. Bowman. 2013. "Acceptance and Commitment Therapy in the Treatment of Anxiety: A Systematic Review." *Clinical Psychology Review* 33(8): 965–978.

Tsai, H. J., T. B. J. Kuo, G.-S. Lee, and C. C. H. Yang. 2015. "Efficacy of Paced Breathing for Insomnia: Enhances Vagal Activity and Improves Sleep Quality." *Psychophysiology* 52(3): 388–396.

Weil, A. 1999. *Breathing: The Master Key to Self-Healing*. Louisville, CO: Sounds True.

Charles Schaeffer, PhD, is a licensed psychologist, and adjunct clinical faculty member at New York University who has been teaching students and patients how to use the latest research to overcome panic, sleep, and anxiety disorders for over a decade. Schaeffer was previously research director and guest host for the *Dr. Fritz Show* on WWRL-AM radio in New York, NY. His writing and expertise have been featured in *Psychology Today*, *HuffPost*, *Vice News*, and *NBC News Health*. He lives in Brooklyn, NY.

Real change *is* possible

For more than forty-five years, New Harbinger has published proven-effective self-help books and pioneering workbooks to help readers of all ages and backgrounds improve mental health and well-being, and achieve lasting personal growth. In addition, our spirituality books offer profound guidance for deepening awareness and cultivating healing, self-discovery, and fulfillment.

Founded by psychologist Matthew McKay and Patrick Fanning, New Harbinger is proud to be an independent, employee-owned company. Our books reflect our core values of integrity, innovation, commitment, sustainability, compassion, and trust. Written by leaders in the field and recommended by therapists worldwide, New Harbinger books are practical, accessible, and provide real tools for real change.

newharbingerpublications